Collins

Cambridge Lower Secondary

English as a Second Language

Anna Cowper

Series Editor: Nick Coates

STAGE 9: WORKBOOK

William Collins' dream of knowledge for all began with the publication of his first book in 1819.

A self-educated mill worker, he not only enriched millions of lives, but also founded a flourishing publishing house. Today, staying true to this spirit, Collins books are packed with inspiration, innovation and practical expertise. They place you at the centre of a world of possibility and give you exactly what you need to explore it.

Collins. Freedom to teach.

Published by Collins
An imprint of HarperCollins*Publishers*
The News Building
1 London Bridge Street
London
SE1 9GF

Browse the complete Collins catalogue at
www.collins.co.uk

© HarperCollins*Publishers* Limited 2017

10 9 8 7 6 5 4 3 2 1

ISBN 978-0-00821548-4

British Library Cataloguing in Publication Data

A catalogue record for this publication is available from the British Library.

Author: Anna Cowper
Development editor: Cait Hawkins
Series Editor: Nick Coates
Commissioning editor: Lucy Cooper
In-house editor: Lara McMurray
Project Manager: Anna Stevenson
Copyeditor: Kelly Davis
Answer checker: Sonya Newland
Proofreader: Karen Williams
Cover designer: Kevin Robbins
Cover illustrator: Maria Herbert-Liew
Typesetter: Jouve India Private Ltd
Production controller: Rachel Weaver
Printed and bound by: Grafica Veneta in Italy

Acknowledgements

The publishers gratefully acknowledge the permission granted to reproduce the copyright material in this book. Every effort has been made to trace copyright holders and to obtain their permission for the use of copyright material. The publishers will gladly receive any information enabling them to rectify any error or omission at the first opportunity.

Key: l = left, r = right, c = centre

p10 Filipe Frazao/Shutterstock, p13 frantic00/ Shutterstock, p16 pbombaert/ Shutterstock, p21 vicvic13/Shutterstock, p28 rdonar/ Shutterstock, p30 Fabio Berti/Shutterstock, p37 wavebreakmedia/Shutterstock, p38 Juthamat89/ Shutterstock, p46l Miissa/Shutterstock, p46cl ANNA ZASIMOVA/Shutterstock, p46cr Zeynur Babayev/Shutterstock, p46r Manon_ Labe/Shutterstock, p48 wavebreakmedia/ Shutterstock, p50 vectorfusionart/Shutterstock, p52 pzAxe/Shutterstock, p55 Anutr Yossundara/ Shutterstock, p57 ImageFlow/Shutterstock, p60 TungCheung/Shutterstock, p64 PrinceOfLove/ Shutterstock, p68 visualpower/Shutterstock, p69 KennyK.com/Shutterstock, p70 Lorelyn Medina/Shutterstock, p72 TypoArt BS/ Shutterstock, p73 tynyuk/Shutterstock, p80 wellphoto/Shutterstock, p83 argus/Shutterstock, p85 LAHI/Shutterstock

MIX
Paper from responsible sources
FSC
www.fsc.org **FSC™ C007454**

This book is produced from independently certified FSC paper to ensure responsible forest management.

For more information visit:
www.harpercollins.co.uk/green

Contents

Connections

Reading: comprehension

SB p.9

Read the text about Lara again and choose the correct answer.

1 She likes spending time on line:
a posting selfies   b meeting people   c writing her fashion blog.

2 If anything makes Lara feel bad when she is talking to people on line, she:
a turns off her computer   b talks to other teenagers about it   c tells her mum.

3 Lara thinks she has a good relationship with Ilinka because they:
a talk a lot   b like the same things   c never have arguments.

4 Lara talks to Jade:
a once or twice a week   b using her own Skype account   c using the family Skype account.

5 Jade is:
a studying at university   b intelligent and funny   c keen on music and art.

Reading: thinking about the text

SB p.9

Answer these questions.

1 What are Lara's hobbies and interests?

_____

2 Why do you think her life online is so important to her?

_____

3 What is Lara's mother's attitude towards her online activities?

_____

4 Does it surprise you?

_____

Vocabulary: words in context

SB p.9

Complete the sentences with the words in the box.

| alternative   constantly   keen on   rarely   relationship   taste |

1 My friend moved to a different city so we _____ see each other now.

2 They are very _____ sport – they spend all their free time playing football and tennis.

3 My friend Julie is a bit _____. She always wears black but dyes her hair different colours!

4 I have a good _____ with my parents. We listen to and respect each other.

5 I'm sorry but you have terrible _____ in music – how can you listen to such awful bands?

6 Please listen to me while I'm speaking and stop _____ checking your phone for messages!

Use of English: tense review

1 **Choose the best word to complete the sentences.**

1 I _____ a new computer soon. My parents have promised to buy me one.
    a get   **b** 'm getting   **c** got

2 Normally, he _____ the bus to school, but today his dad drove him.
    a takes   **b** is taking   **c** is taken by

3 "Have you ever been to America?" "Yes, I have. I _____ my aunt in New York last year."
    a visited   **b** have visited   **c** have been to

4 The computer room _____ by another class at the moment. We can use it this afternoon.
    a is used   **b** is being used   **c** was used

5 "Do you like volleyball?" "I don't know. I _____ it."
    a never played it   **b** never play it   **c** have never played

6 He _____ to bed very late last night. He was playing computer games online until nearly midnight.
    a went   **b** goes   **c** has gone

2 **Complete the text with the verbs in brackets. Use the past simple or present perfect tense.**

My parents [1]_____ (give) me my first phone when I started secondary school

and, since then, I [2]_____ (always have) it with me. I lost it once.

I think it [3]_____ (fall) out of my pocket on the bus and for five whole days

I couldn't talk to my friends, share photos or send funny videos. It was terrible!

I [4]_____ (never feel) so lonely. But I also [5]_____ (notice) that

I had more free time because I [6]_____ (not waste) hours looking at social

media sites and uploading photographs. Since I got my phone back,

I [7]_____ (change) the way I use it. It's still really important for talking to my

friends, but I [8]_____ (stop) spending so much time on the internet.

3 **Complete the sentences with the present simple passive or present continuous passive form of the verb in brackets.**

1 A lot of people are ill at the moment and we don't have enough teachers in the school, so today the children in Year 9 _____ English by computer. (teach)

2 Spanish _____ in many countries in South and Central America as well as in Spain. (speak)

3 Where do you keep this machine when it _____? (not use)

4 Our dinner _____. It will be ready in 10 minutes. (cook)

5 In Japan, the classrooms _____ every day by the children. (clean)

6 The book _____ still _____. The author hasn't finished it yet. (write)

Read the clues and complete the crossword.

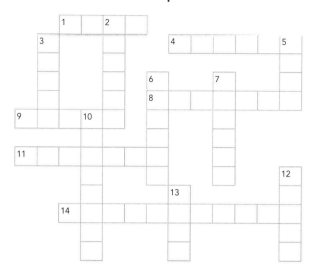

Across

1 To **v**_____ is to make videos about yourself and your life and put them on the internet.

4 A **l**_____ is a thin, light computer with a keyboard, which you can carry.

8 If you have an **a**_____ with an internet company, you can use the services they offer.

9 S_____ makes it possible for people in different places to see and talk to one another on their computers.

11 A **w**_____ is a set of pages of information on the internet about a certain subject.

14 S_____ _____ lets people communicate and share information and pictures on the internet.

Down

2 When you are connected to the internet, you are **o**_____.

3 If you don't want to speak to or receive messages from someone on your computer or your phone, you can **b**_____ him or her.

5 To **p**_____ a photo or a message is to put it on a website so people can see it.

6 A **t**_____ is a very small, light computer that you can hold in your hand.

7 To **f**_____ someone on the internet is to look regularly at the information and pictures they share.

10 Your **p**_____ is a set of letters or numbers that only you know and which lets you open your computer or get into your websites.

12 An **e**_____ is a written message that you send by computer.

13 A **b**_____ is pieces of writing about a person or a subject on the internet.

Vocabulary: describing people

Complete the dialogues with the words in the box.

creative   popular   shy   confident   sociable   sensitive

1

Andrew: Do you know Leo? He's the most ¹_____ boy in the class – everyone wants to be his friend!

Ben: We're in the same group for geography. He's very ²_____, too. He's never nervous about speaking in front of the class.

Andrew: Yes, and he's very ³_____. He loves meeting new people and chatting to

them. I'm not usually keen on people like him because I'm quiet and a bit ⁴_____ so I find it difficult to talk to them, but he's really friendly.

2

Sarah: Rachel is very friendly and she's also the most ⁵_____ person I have ever met. Her bedroom at home is full of amazing paintings on the wall and things she has made.

Liz: Isn't she that tall girl who always dresses in black? I have always been afraid to speak to her!

Sarah: She's a very kind person and very ⁶_____, too. She would be upset if she knew you were afraid of her.

Use of English: questions

1 Complete the questions with the words in the box.

How much   Why   Which   What   Who   What time   Where   How

1 _____ do you like better – travelling by car or by train?

2 _____ does it cost to buy new trainers?

3 _____ are your parents these days?

4 _____ ate all the cakes?

5 _____ did you leave the house?

6 _____ are you phoning from? I can't hear you very well.

7 _____ didn't you wait for us?

8 _____ does she look like?

2 Match the questions from 1 above with these answers (a–h).

a I'm sitting on a bus.
b Josie did.
c She's tall with grey hair.
d They're very well, thank you.
e I prefer the train.
f Because I didn't know you were coming!
g At about 12:30.
h About $60.

3 Complete the indirect questions.

1 Do you know _____?
His name is Jim.

2 Can you tell me _____?
That scarf costs $50.

3 We'd like to know _____.
The restaurant opens at 7:00 p.m.

4 Do you remember _____?
She lives in the next street.

5 I'd be interested to find out _____.
He earns over one hundred thousand dollars a year.

Vocabulary: fibre optics

| cable   protect   reflect   signal   transfer |

Complete the sentences with the words from the box. You may have to change the form of some words.

1 These electronic _____ connect the machines to the central computer.

2 I will _____ the photos from the camera to my computer and email them to you.

3 You can see the sky _____ in the lake.

4 Because the house is surrounded by mountains, we don't get a good internet _____.

5 He wears dark glasses to _____ his eyes from the sun.

Check your progress

1 What can you do now?

I can …

understand a text about how a teenager uses her computer ☐

describe my friends and relationships ☐

listen to and understand an interview with two vloggers ☐

My learning

What did you learn in this unit?

use a variety of present and past tense forms ☐

ask direct and indirect questions ☐

2 Answer the questions about this unit.

1 What have you learned?

_____

2 Is there anything you have found difficult?

_____

3 What would you like to learn more about?

_____

Reading: comprehension
SB p.19

Read the text again and decide if the sentences are true or false or whether it doesn't say.

1 Tuwe is an important person in his tribe. True / False / Doesn't say
2 Tuwe had travelled by plane before. True / False / Doesn't say
3 He believed that his soul arrived in the city after his body. True / False / Doesn't say
4 Using public transport in New York was frightening for Tuwe. True / False / Doesn't say
5 Learning how to use technology was difficult for him. True / False / Doesn't say
6 He wants to teach people about plants and medicines. True / False / Doesn't say

Reading: thinking about the text
SB p.19

Answer the questions with your own ideas.

1 What is Tuwe's attitude towards modern technology?

_____

_____

2 Does Tuwe think his culture is less advanced than American culture? Why? Why not?

_____

_____

Vocabulary: words in context

Complete the sentences with the words from the box.

| confidently | duty | headdress | messenger | rainforest |

1 Plants grow very quickly in the _____ because it is so wet and so warm.

2 We must look after the plants and animals in the world: it is our _____ to keep them safe for the future.

3 The members of the tribe don't usually wear many clothes, but some of the men wear a

special _____ on their heads to show how important they are.

4 Some technology is new to the people in the village but after a short time they use

it _____.

5 The chief of the tribe sent a _____ to tell us that he didn't accept our offer.

Use of English: abstract nouns

SB p.19

1 Complete the table with words from the text.

abstract noun	adjective / adverb / verb
confidence	[1]confidently
happiness	[2]_____
tiredness	[3]_____
[4]_____	to know

2 Choose the correct abstract noun to complete the sentences.

1 He lived in France for a long time and has a good [confidence / knowledge] of the French language.

2 I feel true [happiness / tiredness] when I'm with my friends and the people I love.

3 When I know I have studied hard, I have a feeling of [confidence / knowledge] when I go into an exam: I know I will do my best.

4 Even if you sleep a lot, the feeling of [happiness / tiredness] that you get after a long journey by plane usually lasts for several days.

Use of English: the –*ing* form

SB p.20

1 Complete the sentences with the –*ing* form of the verbs in the box. There are two verbs that you do not need.

> get   leave   make   meet   teach   speak   study   travel

1 Tuwe has left the village before, but _____ his family always makes him sad.

2 _____ by plane for the first time was an exciting experience.

3 Tuwe had always wanted to study film-_____.

4 _____ the other students on his course was something that he enjoyed a lot.

5 _____ used to cold weather was not easy for him. He had to buy warm clothes.

6 He believes that _____ other people about his culture is his duty.

2 Which two verbs from the box were not used in activity 1 above? Write sentences using the –*ing* form of these two verbs.

1 _____

2 _____

Vocabulary: life events

SB p.21

Complete the sentences with the words in the box. Make sure you use the correct form of the verb.

> be born   get married   have children   marry   retire   train

1 We are going to _____ after Christmas in my home town. We want a small, quiet wedding.

2 Your mother and I got married two years before you _____.

3 He's over sixty and he's worked here all his life; I expect he's going to _____ soon.

4 He _____ a girl who he met when he was working in France. They seem very happy together and are expecting a baby.

5 He _____ to be an engineer when the war broke out, but he gave up his studies to join the army.

6 Although he said he had never really wanted to _____, my uncle was very happy when my cousin was born.

> *Vocabulary tip*
>
> **to marry** (someone)   vs   **to get married** (no object)
>
> Francis *married John*.   They *got married* in August.

Reading: my grandmothers

SB p.21

Match the beginnings (1–6) and the endings (a–f) to make sentences about Rosa's grandmothers.

1 My grandmothers were

2 Shima's parents both died when she was a baby,

3 Marilee's family was quite rich and she was

4 Both my grandmothers got married

5 Shima trained as a teacher at the same time

6 Marilee started her own taxi business

a the youngest child, so she had everything she wanted.

b which became very successful.

c and had children when they were young.

d as she was bringing up her five daughters!

e born in the same year – 1948, in the state of Arizona in the USA.

f but luckily an aunt looked after her.

Use of English: past tenses revision

SB p.22

Write complete sentences. One of the underlined verbs must be in the past simple and the other underlined verb in the past perfect *or* the past continuous tense.

1 While my grandfather / <u>grow up</u> / there <u>be</u> / lots of problems / in our country.

  While my grandfather was growing up, there were lots of problems in our country.

2 Before he / <u>go</u> away / to school, / he <u>never visit</u> / a big city.

  _____

3 He <u>get</u> interested in / nature and plants / while / he <u>live</u> in the mountains.

  _____

4 He <u>just start</u> /studying at university / when the war / <u>begin</u>.

  _____

5 He <u>learn</u> to speak Chinese / while / he <u>work</u> in China.

  _____

6 Although / my grandfather / <u>never leave</u> the country before, / he <u>find</u> / he loved travelling and working abroad.

  _____

Vocabulary: celebrations

SB p.23

Complete the sentences about a celebration with suitable words. The first letter of each word is given. All the words can be found on page 23 in the Student's Book.

1 My cousin is going to get married. Her

  w_____ will be in the summer.

2 Her f_____ is from a family who like to

  do things in the t_____ way, so there's going to be a really big party!

3 In my country it's the family of the b_____, not the bride, who pay for everything.

4 During the c_____, the couple exchange rings and promise to look after each other.

5 Afterwards, there is a big f_____ – the eating and drinking usually goes on for two days.

6 People usually invite all their r_____ to the party, so if you have a big family

  there will be lots of g_____.

1 Match the beginnings (1–6) and the endings (a–f) to complete this list of events.

1 We have guests coming tomorrow. First, I'll decide what we're going to eat. _____b_____

2 Start by making a list of all the people you want to invite, _____

3 We danced all night under the stars _____

4 The first thing you should do when your guests arrive is to introduce them to people they don't know. _____

5 Firstly, make sure you have a good sound system and that it is working properly; _____

6 I served all the guests food and drink _____

a Next, you should offer them something to drink.

b After that, I'll go to the shops and buy the food.

c and, last of all, I served myself.

d and finally went to bed when the sun was rising.

e secondly, choose some good music that you know people will enjoy listening to.

f then decide if you are going to post invitations or send them by email.

2 Underline all the words used in activity 1 above to put events in order. Note that we put a comma after these words if they come at the beginning of a phrase or sentence.

Check your progress

1 What can you do now?

I can …

understand and talk about life events and family history ☐

tell a story using a range of past narrative tenses ☐

use the –*ing* form as a noun ☐

write about a family celebration or special event ☐

read, understand and discuss an extract from a story ☐

2 Answer the questions about this unit.

1 What have you enjoyed most?

_____

2 Is there anything you have found difficult?

_____

3 What would you like to learn more about?

_____

My learning

What did you learn in this unit?

3 Room

Reading: comprehension SB p.31

Read the text again and choose the correct answer.

1 Lots of people want to live in Dharavi because _____.
   a it's cheap   b it's easy to find a place to live   c no rich people live there

2 _____ people live in Lakshmi's house.
   a Four   b Five   c Six

3 Because their house is so small, Lakshmi's family is very _____.
   a tidy   b hot   c messy

4 Inside Lakshmi's house, it is _____.
   a cool and dark   b hot and dark   c small and light

5 The house has _____.
   a water but no electricity   b electricity and water   c electricity but no water

6 Tourists come to Dharavi to _____.
   a help the people who live there   b learn about recycling   c buy things

Reading: thinking about the text SB p.31

Answer the questions.

1 Is there anything that surprises you about Lakshmi's house? Why? Why not?

_____

2 Why do you think the people in Dharavi are so good at recycling things?

_____

Vocabulary: words in context SB p.32

Complete the sentences with the words from the box. You may have to change the form of some words.

| running water | narrow | recycle | waste | tap | possessions |

1 There isn't enough space in my room for all my _____.

2 Soon we will have a proper bathroom with _____ in our house and I'll be able to take a shower.

3 The bottles will be _____ and the glass will be used to make windows.

4 Forgetting to turn off the light when you leave the room is a _____ of electricity.

5 She turned on the _____ and hot water came out.

6 They built the bridge over the _____ part of the river.

Vocabulary: phrases with *and*

SB p.32

Match the beginnings (1–5) and the endings (a–e) to make sentences.

1 You can take your coat and scarf off
2 Your bedroom looks different
3 Try one of these apples
4 This carpet is nice and soft
5 Your hair is lovely and shiny

a – they're lovely and juicy.
b – I love how it feels under my feet.
c – what kind of shampoo do you use?
d – it's lovely and warm in here!
e – it's nice and tidy for once!

Use of English: talking about quantity

SB p.32

1 **Choose the best phrase to complete the sentences.**

1 There aren't [too much / very many / so much] houses with running water.

2 We have [so little / such little /so few] time and so much to do!

3 There are [very little / so small number of / very few] recycling centres.

4 Unfortunately, most of this rubbish is thrown away: [too few / very few / too little] is recycled.

5 I think we have wasted [a small amount / a great deal of / a large number of] time talking and now we should start doing something.

6 If people continue to leave [large amounts / large numbers / very much] of rubbish in the street, the area will never get better.

2 **Complete the sentences with the phrases from the box.**

Too many	too little	Very few of	too much	deal of	amount of

1 I think he put _____ sugar in this. It's terribly sweet!

2 _____ the young people I met are going to stay in the area. Most will move to the city.

3 If there's _____ water in the pot, the plant will get dry and then die. Make sure you give it some water every day.

4 There's only a small _____ coffee left. I'll go and buy some more.

5 _____ children don't know how to cook! Most of them can't even boil an egg.

6 By the time we've paid the bills, there isn't a great _____ money left to spend on going out and having fun.

Use of English: *both, either, neither, each, several, none*

SB p.34

Choose the best words to complete the sentences.

1 Most people are [either / neither] rich or happy, but not both.

2 There were [several / none] people who said they were interested, but in the end [one / none] of them decided to do it.

3 I haven't met [either / neither] of his sisters, but people say that they are [both / neither] nice girls.

4 [Neither / Either] Tim nor his brother like tidying their room.

5 He invited [each / both] of the three boys to play on the team and, for various reasons, [none / neither] of them was able to come.

6 It's [either / neither] on the table in the living room or I left it in my bag – I can't remember which.

7 There were [several / none] houses for sale and we visited [each / either] of them.

8 [Both / Neither] of us are learning English, but [neither / both] of us has been to an English-speaking country yet.

Vocabulary: multiword verbs

SB p.33

1 **Match these multiword verbs (1–5) with their correct meanings (a–e).**

1 tidy up   **a** to put something in the place where you usually keep it

2 give away   **b** to make a place or collection of things tidy

3 put away   **c** to give something to somebody without asking for payment

4 fit into   **d** what you do with something you don't want any more – either putting it in the rubbish or giving it to another person

5 get rid of   **e** to be able to be or go into a place because it's big enough and there is enough space

2 **Complete these sentences with verbs from activity 1 above. You may have to change the form of some words.**

1 Nobody wanted to buy the chairs, so in the end he _____ them _____ to a school.

2 My bookshelves are full, but I don't want to _____ books so I keep them.

3 All my clothes used to _____ one small chest of drawers, but they don't any more!

4 Their room was in a terrible mess and I told them to _____ it _____ immediately.

5 It was the end of the lesson and the children were _____ their books.

Reading: a conversation

SB p.34

Match Ann's questions (1–5) with Enid's responses (a–e).

Ann:

1 What do you think of my room?

2 You're right, I do have a lot of stuff but so do you.

3 Really?

4 Was it difficult?

5 So you think I should do it?

Enid:

a At first it was but now I have more space and feel much happier.

b That's not true, I don't have half as much as you.

c Why not? I'll help you.

d Yes, I did the 49 Things Challenge and got rid of loads of stuff.

e You have far too much stuff. I think you should do the 49 Things Challenge.

Use of English: *so do I, neither do I, I don't either*

SB p.34

Read the *Language tip*, then complete the sentences with the phrases from the box.

> **Language tip**
>
> *so do I, neither do I, either* for agreeing and disagreeing
>
> **Agreeing:** *so* + auxiliary verb + subject
>
> I like swimming. **So do I.**   I learned to swim when I was young. **So did I.**
>
> **Disagreeing:** *neither* + auxiliary verb + subject
>
> I don't like swimming. **Neither do I.**   I didn't learn to swim at school. **Neither did I.**
>
> **Disagreeing:** auxiliary verb + *either*
>
> I don't like swimming. I don't **either.**   I didn't learn to swim at school. I didn't **either.**

| didn't either   don't either   neither did you   do I   doesn't either   Neither do we |

1 "You didn't tidy your room today." "That's true, but _____!"

2 "I want to go to the library later." "So _____. Let's go together."

3 "Their house doesn't have running water." "That's not unusual in this area;

   ours _____."

4 "We don't always recycle our rubbish." "Don't feel too bad about it. _____."

5 "I think the new building is really ugly and I don't like it." "I _____. It's awful."

6 "I didn't understand the last part of the geometry lesson." "We _____.
   Shall we ask the teacher for help?"

Vocabulary: describing a room

Read the clues and complete the crossword.

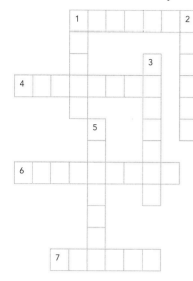

Across

1 areas on the edge of a town or city where many people live

4 a large, tall cupboard you can hang clothes in

6 a set of rooms for living in which are on one floor of a building

7 a space usually filled with glass in the wall of a building where light comes in

Down

1 a room for working or studying in

2 people use these to go up or down in a building (on foot)

3 the part of a room that is above your head

5 a room where people prepare and cook food

Check your progress

1 What can you do now?

I can …

read and understand a text about how someone lives ☐

discuss my attitudes to tidiness and untidiness ☐

use a range of different expressions to express quantity ☐

understand people talking about their possessions ☐

understand a text about geometry ☐

negotiate, plan and present ideas about how to use a shared space ☐

2 Answer the questions about this unit.

1 What have you enjoyed most?

_____

2 Is there anything you have found difficult?

_____

3 What would you like to learn more about?

_____

My learning

What did you learn in this unit?

4 Getting around

Vocabulary: transport

SB p.40

Add as many words as you can to the mind map. Add more words as you go through the unit.

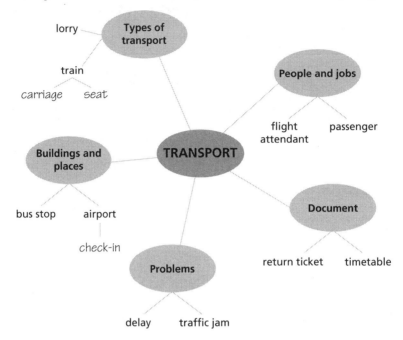

Vocabulary: words in context

Complete the sentences with the words from the box. You may have to change the form of some words.

> cycle lane   helmet   rush hour   spread out   system   traffic jam

1 There is a great network of _____ across the city so you can travel anywhere by bike.

2 We have a really good public transport _____: you can get to any part of town by bus, train or tram.

3 It's important to protect your head with a _____ if you're a cyclist or motorcyclist.

4 The morning _____ begins around 8:00 a.m. because that's the time when most people are driving to work.

5 We're stuck in a long line of cars that haven't moved forward for over an hour; it's the worst _____ I've ever seen.

6 To the south of the city is a large forest which _____ across the whole valley. It takes an hour to drive through it.

Use of English: sentence adverbs

SB p.41

Complete the sentences with the sentence adverbs from the box. You can use each adverb more than once, if necessary.

> certainly   especially   mostly   particularly   unfortunately

1 I love cycling round the city, _particularly_ in warm, sunny weather.

2 _____, there was an accident which meant the trains were delayed.

3 The public transport here is very good, _____ the excellent bus system.

4 Sometimes my parents drive me to school, but _____ I walk.

5 _____, the cost of public transport is higher than it was in the past.

6 _____ I feel very safe travelling by bike since there are lots of cycle lanes.

Reading: comprehension

SB p.43

1 **Read the text again and decide if the sentences are true or false.**

  1 Camels like to walk one behind another.   True / False

  2 Getting on a camel is easy.   True / False

  3 Your camel might be taller than you.   True / False

  4 Camel riders mostly use their legs to control their camels.   True / False

  5 There will be time every day for the camels to wash themselves in the river.   True / False

  6 If you surprise a camel, it might kick you.   True / False

2 **Correct the false sentences in 1 above.**

_____

_____

_____

_____

Reading: thinking about the text

SB p.43

Answer the questions.

1 What would you enjoy the most and the least about riding a camel?

_____

2 Why did the writer write this text? What do you think he/she hopes will happen as a result of people reading it?

_____

Vocabulary: words in context

SB p.43

1 **Complete the sentences with the words from the box. You may have to change the form of some words.**

control	gentle	in single file	make faces	sudden	tightly

1 He's a funny boy who keeps _____ and telling jokes to make the other children laugh.

2 The path was so narrow we had to walk _____.

3 There was a _____ storm in the afternoon: it started so quickly that there was no time to bring the things in from the garden.

4 When you first start driving, it takes time to learn to _____ the car.

5 Please hold my hand _____ and don't let go – I'm afraid of losing you.

2 **Which word from the box was not used? Use this word to write a sentence of your own.**

_____

Use of English: future continuous

SB p.44

1 **Complete the sentences with the verbs from the box in the correct future continuous form.**

climb	drive	have	not go	not walk	ride	swim

1 Tomorrow we _____ in the sea in the warm sunshine.

2 When they go on their trip to the Sahara next month, they _____ across the desert. They _____ camels.

3 My brother is going on an adventure camp, so next week he _____ a mountain in Italy.

4 _____ you _____ Spanish lessons before your visit to Mexico next year?

5 He _____ to bed early this evening. It's his birthday and he's going to have a party.

6 Mum is going to meet your aunt at the airport this afternoon. She _____ there later.

2 Choose the best verb form to complete the sentences.

1 My parents [will be waiting / will wait] for me when I arrive.

2 If you ask Jane, she [will help / will be helping] you with your homework – she's good at maths.

3 My father [will work / will be working] in his restaurant at 10 o'clock tonight.

4 Don't come at seven – we ['ll have / 'll be having] dinner then. Come at 7:30.

5 "We've missed the bus." "Never mind I ['ll be walking / 'll walk] home."

6 "Will you come shopping with us on Saturday?" "I'm sorry, I can't.
I ['ll be playing / 'll play] football all day – I'm in the school team."

7 Did you buy some ice cream? I ['ll put / 'll be putting] it in the freezer.

8 Every evening next week she ['ll study / 'll be studying] for her exams.

Use of English: mixed future forms

SB p.44

1 Match the examples (1–4) with the verb form explanations (a–d).

1 It'll rain tomorrow, I'm sure it will.

2 It's going to rain any moment now – look at those clouds.

3 We're meeting in front of the school at 3:30, unless it rains.

4 The weather forecast for tomorrow is terrible – we'll be walking for miles in the pouring rain.

a *going to* + verb for future plans and events in the near future when there are signs now that they are going to happen

b *will* + *be* + *–ing* (future continuous) to talk about situations that are still continuing at a certain time in the future

c present continuous for future plans and arrangements, often with a date or time

d will + verb for predictions about the future (when a continuous action is not being described)

2 Complete the sentences with the verb in brackets. Use the best future form of the verb from 1 above. (Sometimes more than one correct answer is possible.)

1 **A:** What's the matter?

B: I feel terrible. I think I _____ sick. (be)

2 **A:** You look scared. What are you thinking about?

B: I'm thinking about tomorrow. Tomorrow night, we _____ to walk on stage! (get ready)

3 **A:** So what are your plans for tomorrow?

B: We _____ the others at 9 o'clock at the bus station. (meet)

4 **A:** Shall we walk or take the bus on Saturday?

B: We should definitely take the bus. I listened to the weather forecast and

it _____ all day. (rain)

Complete the email with the words from the box.

| accommodation | attractions | destination | museums |
| self-catering | sightseeing | sites |

To:

From:

Dear Annie

I'm looking forward to my holiday in Barcelona. It's an exciting ¹_____, near both the sea and the mountains, with lots of tourist ²_____ too – like great beaches, shops and restaurants. It's a historic city as well, with lots of amazing ³_____, full of beautiful and old things. My dad loves ⁴_____: he likes to visit as many old buildings and historic ⁵_____ as possible. My mum's ideal holiday ⁶_____ is a hotel, but we've rented a ⁷_____ place this year because we like to be independent. We've promised Mum that we'll do all the cooking!

Jay

Check your progress

My learning

1 What can you do now?

What did you learn in this unit?

I can …

understand people talking about travel and transport ☐

use sentence adverbs ☐

understand a text about how to ride a camel ☐

use the future continuous tense ☐

talk and write about holiday and travel plans ☐

2 Answer the questions about this unit.

1 What have you enjoyed most?

_____

2 Is there anything you have found difficult?

_____

3 What would you like to learn more about?

_____

5 Tourism

Vocabulary: words in context

SB p.52

Complete the conversation with the words from the box. You may have to change the form of some words.

| benefit | block | damage | employment | expect | ruin | weigh up |

Anne: Do you really think tourism has ¹_____ the island and made it a terrible place?

Winston: Sometimes I do, yes. When I look at the crowded beaches, the roads ²_____ with traffic and the ugly new hotels, I hate the tourists. The hotel swimming pools use too much water and are ³_____ the environment. On the other hand, my café makes lots of money in the summer while the tourists are here.

Anne: Yes, simply hating tourism would be stupid! I think we should ⁴_____ the good and bad points carefully. Look how many local people work in the tourist hotels and restaurants, for example. The tourism industry certainly creates a lot of ⁵_____.

Winston: Yes, but if you work for the local tourist industry, you can't ⁶_____ to have a job all the year round. There's only enough work for everyone in the summer.

Anne: And some people earn so much money in the summer, they don't need to work for four months of the year! I agree that tourism certainly has its disadvantages but there are ⁷_____ too.

Vocabulary: tourists

SB p.53

Match a verb in Box A with a word or phrase in Box B to complete the sentences.

A

| cause | create | depend on |
| fill | leave | put up |

B

| jobs | rubbish | the cafés and restaurants |
| their prices | tourism | traffic jams |

1 Tourism is good for local businesses: in the summer it's the tourists who _____ _____, and make money for local people.

2 One of the reasons why people _____ _____ on the beach is because there aren't any bins there.

3 It's true that the owners of the shops and restaurants _____ _____ in the summer and we all have to pay more.

4 Local people don't work as farmers or fishermen any more; they _____ _____ to earn money to support their families.

5 In the summer, coaches full of tourists _____ _____ in the old town because the roads are not wide enough for them to pass.

6 The new amusement park and adventure sports centre will attract more tourists to the area and _____ _____ for young people.

1   Match the beginnings (1–7) and the endings (a–g) to make sentences.

1   I don't know why he was chosen for the athletics team and not me. I can run   _b_

2   If you want to pass the exam, you will have to work _____

3   I'm sorry my note was difficult to read. Next time, I'll make sure I write _____

4   I thought Jim was the worst dancer in the world, but Greg dances _____

5   We thought we would hardly ever see her after she moved further away, but she visits us _____

6   I'm trying to get to sleep. Could you try to be _____

7   This time, she listened to me _____

a   a bit more patiently.

b   just as fast.

c   slightly less noisy?

d   much harder.

e   slightly more often.

f   a bit more carefully.

g   just as badly.

2   Complete the dialogues with a comparative adverb. Use the underlined adverb and make it stronger, using *slightly, a bit, just as, much, a lot or less*.

1   **A:** How's Julie. Is she working <u>hard</u> these days?

     B: Well she's studying *a bit harder* than she did last year, but I think she could do better!

2   **A:** Do you think you will finish the job in time? Can you work <u>fast</u> enough?

     B: Since we've had the new machines, we have been able to work _____. We get nearly twice as much done!

3   **A:** Are we nearly at the top? Will we have to walk <u>far</u>?

     B: Well, it looks as if we'll have to walk _____ than we thought, but only a couple of kilometres.

4   **A:** I need someone to come with me and be a translator. How <u>well</u> does Lily speak Chinese?

     B: She's speaks it _____ since her trip to Beijing. Her teacher can't believe how much she has improved.

5   **A:** Did you tell the teacher that you can't hear her and ask her to speak less <u>quietly</u>?

     B: Yes, I did but it makes no difference. She speaks _____ as she did before.

6   **A:** Do you <u>often</u> visit your grandparents in France?

     B: The flights have become very expensive so we still go to see them when we can but we visit _____ than in the past.

Reading: comprehension

SB p.54

1 Read the text again and decide if the sentences are true or false.

1 Local people don't always earn money from tourists.   True / False

2 Tourists can make local people feel like objects.   True / False

3 Local people manage community-based tourism.   True / False

4 Tourists can't go inside the houses of local people.   True / False

5 Community-based tourism creates respect for traditional ways of life.   True / False

6 The money from community-based tourism is used to build better hotels.   True / False

2 Correct the false sentences.

_____

_____

Reading: thinking about the text

SB p.54

Answer the questions.

1 According to the text, what are typical activities in mass tourism? What activities can community-based tourists do?

_____

_____

2 How is the relationship between local people and tourists different in community-based tourism?

_____

_____

Vocabulary: words in context

SB p.55

Complete the sentences with the words from the box.

income	provide	respect	response	service	stare

1 I tried not to _____, but I couldn't stop looking at the children – they were so beautiful!

2 We don't have a large _____ even though we work hard; our jobs are not well paid.

3 The _____ in the hotels is excellent; everybody is polite and friendly.

4 If we want tourists to come here, we need to _____ things to do and places to stay.

5 We asked the local people about the project and their _____ was very positive.

6 Tourists should _____ the local culture. If they aren't interested in it, why are they here?

Use of English: present perfect simple and continuous   SB p.55

Choose the best verb form to complete the sentences.

1 They [have been building / have built] new hotels for all the extra tourists since last year, but none of them are finished yet.

2 I [have been writing / have written] five emails this morning and now I'm going to stop for lunch.

3 He ['s painted / 's been painting] the kitchen, but there isn't quite enough paint so he's gone to buy some more.

4 My brother's been in the school football team for two years and they [have won / have been winning] two cups so far.

5 I ['ve washed / 've been washing] the car, but it's really dirty so I need to fetch another bucket of water!

Use of English: past perfect continuous   SB p.56

1 Complete the sentences with the verb in brackets. Use the past perfect continuous form.

1 I _____ a film before I went to bed. (watch)

2 The tourists _____ the museum when their bags went missing. (visit)

3 She _____ well all morning. (not feel)

4 We _____ long before the train arrived. (not wait)

5 They _____ football all day and were so tired that they fell asleep during dinner. (play)

6 What _____ before the teacher came into the classroom? (they / do)

2 Complete the sentences with the correct form of the verb in brackets. Use the past perfect or the past perfect continuous.

1 Before I came to live here I _____ never _____ a mountain in my life! (climb)

2 She _____ for a long time and was feeling very tired. (walk)

3 I _____ wood all afternoon but I hadn't filled the lorry. (cut)

4 They were astonished when they saw the valley: they _____ never _____ such a beautiful place. (see)

5 He _____ just _____ the tent when it started raining, so we both quickly got inside. (put up)

Vocabulary: describing a place

SB p.57

1 Match the sets of adjectives (a–f) and the natural features (1–6) they describe.

a clear, sparkling	**b** bright blue	**c** long, green
d shining golden	**e** cool, shady	**f** high, rocky

1 _e_ forest	**2** _____ sands	**3** _____ mountains
4 _____ stream	**5** _____ sky	**6** _____ grass

2 Complete the sentences with the adjective + noun combinations from activity 1 above.

1 We walk under the trees in the _cool, shady forest_.

2 I love to watch the _____ and listen to the musical sound of the water.

3 I like lying down in the _____ of the hillside and looking up at the

_____ .

4 They looked towards the _____ and saw that there was already snow at the top.

5 When we arrive at the beach, I take off my shoes and run across the

_____ to the sea.

Check your progress

1 What can you do now?

I can ...

talk and write about tourism ☐

compare with adverbs ☐

understand and use continuous forms ☐

write a description of my favourite place ☐

plan and present a tour ☐

2 Answer the questions about this unit.

1 What have you enjoyed most?

_____

2 Is there anything you have found difficult?

_____

3 What would you like to learn more about?

_____

My learning

What did you learn in this unit?

6 The brain

Reading: comprehension

SB p.62

Read the text again and choose the best way to complete the sentences (a or b).

1 Dr John Medina has discovered
   a some rules about how our brains work.
   b how memory and sleep control our brains.

2 The sense that helps our brains most when we are trying to remember things is
   a sight.
   b hearing.

3 We can also improve our memory by
   a learning songs and maths formulas.
   b repeating things to ourselves.

4 Many people feel tired in the middle of the afternoon because
   a there are chemicals in our brain that want us to sleep.
   b our brains are tired.

5 Having a sleep in the afternoon can help us
   a get more things done.
   b become more intelligent.

6 It is better for our brains
   a to change between tasks.
   b to do one task at a time.

Reading: thinking about the text

SB p.62

Answer the questions.

What have you learned from the text about:

1 How to improve your memory?

_____

_____

2 How to get more things done?

_____

_____

Vocabulary: words in context

SB p.63

Complete the sentences with the words from the box. You may have to change the form of some words.

| develop | imagine | memory | rest | sense | sight | stick | yawn |

1 I have noticed that my _____ is getting worse as I get older – I can never remember people's names!

2 I quite often take a _____ in the afternoon if I feel really tired.

3 His _____ isn't very good: when he's sitting at the back of the classroom, he can't read what's on the board.

4 We have five _____ in all but I think seeing and hearing are the most important.

5 Although I can understand a lot, I can't say much; I really want to _____ my speaking skills in English.

6 It is difficult to _____ what the world will be like in the future.

7 I feel really sleepy and I keep _____.

8 I'm trying to remember these new words but they just won't _____ in my head!

Vocabulary: word building

SB p.63

1 Complete the table. You can use a dictionary, if necessary.

Noun	Adjective	Verb
power	1 _____	
connection	connected	2 _____
3 _____	imaginative	imagine
4 _____	developed	develop

2 Complete the dialogue with the words in the table in activity 1 above.

Lisa: I've just heard a really interesting talk about memory and the brain. The man said that repeating things – saying them over and over out loud – is a very [1]_____ way of helping you to remember them.

Jake: Really? That's good to know!

Lisa: Yes, there is also a strong [2]_____ between seeing things and remembering them. If you see a picture of something, you are much more likely to remember it.

Jake: That's interesting too, but what I'd really like to know is how to become more [3]_____ and think of new ideas. That's the skill I'd most like to [4]_____.

Use of English: relative pronouns and clauses

1 **Choose the best word to complete the sentences.**

1 What did you do with the money [whose / that / who] I gave you?

2 Our maths teacher, [which / that / who] is nearly 65 years old, is going to retire next year.

3 I had an argument with the boy [whose / who / which] parents are friends with the head teacher.

4 Thank you for your email, [that / whose / which] was very interesting

5 Ask the girl [who / whose / which] books are still on her desk to put them away.

6 Our school, [who / which / that] is considered the best in the area, has far too many students.

7 My brother is the kind of person [who / which / whose] you can trust.

8 The exam, [which / that / who] was very difficult, lasted for nearly three hours!

2 **Write complete sentences with a relative clause and the pronoun which. Don't forget to add commas.**

1 I / have just run / a five-kilometre-race / was / very tiring.

 I have just run a five-kilometre race, which was very tiring.

2 I / passed / the English exam /made my parents happy.

 _____

3 My grandparents / have just given me / 50 dollars / was / generous of them.

 _____

4 We / have to get up / at 4:00 a.m to go to airport / is the earliest / I've ever got up / in my life!

 _____

5 My cousin / drives / his motorbike / much too fast / is / dangerous / both / for him / and for other people.

 _____

6 Next year / we / are going to New York for Christmas / I'm looking forward to / very much.

 _____

3 **Read the Language tip. Then join the sentences to make one longer sentence. Don't forget to put the preposition at the end of the relative clause.**

> **Language tip**
>
> In a relative clause that contains **adjective + preposition** or **verb + preposition**, the **preposition** goes at the end of the clause.
>
> *Look, there's **the girl who** you were talking **about**.*
>
> *I'll get you **the book that** you were interested **in**.*

1 I was sitting on a chair. The chair broke.

 The chair that I was *sitting on broke*.

2 You told me about a book. It was very interesting.

The book that you _____

3 The teacher was angry with those students. They had arrived very late

The students who the teacher was _____

4 You were looking at a picture. It is by a famous artist.

The picture _____

5 I was worried about that exam. It was the one I got the best marks in.

The exam _____

6 The girl was frightened of the dog. It ran across the road.

The dog _____

Use of English: comparing

SB p.65

Complete the sentences with the comparative forms of the adjectives and adverbs in brackets. Use far, much, more or a lot to make the comparatives stronger.

1 His new film is _much funnier_ than the last one. We laughed and laughed. (funny)

2 If you want people to remember something, showing them pictures is

_____ than just telling them. (powerful)

3 It doesn't help us to try to stay awake if we feel very tired; it's _____ for us to take a nap. (good)

4 TV cameras make people look _____ than they are in real life. (small and fat)

5 In the future, the climate is likely to be _____ than it is now (hot and dry).

6 For long journeys, train travel is _____ than going by car. (fast and comfortable)

Writing: giving advice

SB p.66

Match the solutions from Box A with the advice phrases from Box B. (There is more than one possible phrase you can use in each case.) Then write answers to the problems (1–6).

A

play computer games before bedtime   spend so much time in the gym

multitask   take a rest   ask what the problem is

listen to music to help you think about other things

B

> Why don't you …   You shouldn't …   You ought to …   It's (not) a good idea to …
>
> You need to …   don't …   It's not necessary to …

1 I often text and chat to my friends online as I'm doing my homework but I notice my marks are going down at school.

You shouldn't multitask. Don't try to do more than one thing at once.

2 I feel really tired in the afternoons.

_____

3 My best friend isn't speaking to me.

_____

4 I find it difficult to get to sleep at night.

_____

5 I get very nervous before exams.

_____

6 I've been exercising for two hours every day, and now I feel really tired.

_____

Check your progress

1 What can you do now?

I can …

talk and write about how the brain works ☐

use relative pronouns ☐

understand an interview with someone who had a brain injury ☐

use different structures to make comparisons ☐

give advice in speech and writing ☐

2 Answer the questions about this unit.

1 What have you enjoyed most?

_____

2 Is there anything you have found difficult?

_____

3 What would you like to learn more about?

_____

My learning
What did you learn in this unit?

Food

Vocabulary: sushi

SB p.74

Read the text again. Then find the words in the wordsearch to complete the sentences (1–8).

f	i	s	h	k	a	j	a	p	a	n	y
o	l	p	l	i	r	u	b	l	r	e	o
r	a	i	n	m	o	l	u	m	i	n	a
a	s	c	h	o	p	s	t	i	c	k	s
s	h	y	d	r	o	o	s	t	e	n	e
l	i	f	r	i	e	y	p	o	n	s	a
i	d	g	a	p	r	s	l	i	m	a	w
m	e	v	w	a	s	a	b	i	t	o	e
y	o	e	n	r	c	u	l	a	n	d	e
o	c	r	a	o	k	c	s	u	p	i	d
u	r	g	i	n	g	e	r	a	s	t	o

1 Sushi comes from [1] *Japan.*

2 Sushi is made of boiled [2]_____ and pieces of [3]_____.

3 You don't cook sushi. It is eaten [4]_____.

4 Because of this, some people don't like sushi; they think sushi has a [5]_____ feel.

5 People usually eat sushi with a sauce called [6]_____, thin pieces of [7]_____ and a green paste called [8]_____.

6 These two last things, especially the green paste, are hot and [9]_____.

7 You can eat sushi with your fingers or you can use [10]_____.

8 There is a type of sushi which is covered in [11]_____ on the outside. This is called a Maki roll.

Reading: comprehension

SB p.74

Read the text again and decide if the sentences are true or false or it doesn't say.

1 You can find sushi restaurants in most places but sushi is only really popular in Asia.   True / False / Doesn't say

2 Sushi is usually expensive.   True / False / Doesn't say

3 In most sushi restaurants, there are not many different types of sushi to choose from.   True / False / Doesn't say

4 In very traditional Japanese sushi restaurants, the sushi chef tells the customer which are the freshest fish.   True / False / Doesn't say

5 There is only one way to eat sushi.   True / False / Doesn't say

6 People don't often eat wasabi by itself: they mix it with soy sauce.   True / False / Doesn't say

Reading: thinking about the text

SB p.74

Answer the questions.

1 Why do some people not enjoy eating sushi or want to try it?

_____

_____

2 Do you think sushi is healthy and good for you? Why? Why not?

_____

_____

Vocabulary: words in context

SB p.75

Complete the dialogue with the words from the box.

dip	experience	portions	selection	traditional	variety

A: I have never been in a sushi restaurant before, so this is a completely new

   ¹_____ for me. Could you explain what sushi is exactly?

B: It's a ²_____ Japanese dish which is very old but has become a popular fast food!

   Basically, it's a snack made of small ³_____ of rice and fish. Look, here's the menu.

A: OK, I see. There are pictures of everything. They look delicious and there is a lot of

   ⁴_____ too. I didn't know there would be so many different types.

B: Yes, this restaurant has a good ⁵_____ and there is lots of choice.

A: And what are these little dishes on the table for?

B: Soy sauce. People like to ⁶_____ their sushi in some soy sauce before eating it.

Use of English: *neither ... nor* and *not only ... but also ...*

SB p.76

Put the words and phrases in the correct order to make complete sentences.

1 in that café / but they / They not only / very friendly. / serve great food / are also/

   They not only serve great food in that café but they are also very friendly.

2 very warm. / neither very tasty / Unfortunately, / the soup was / nor

   _____

3 a great cook. / really well, but / she's also / the piano / She not only / plays

   _____

4 He neither said hello / if we wanted / when we came in / a table. / nor asked

   _____

Use of English: *rather*

SB p.76

Complete the dialogue with an adjective from the box and *rather* or *rather a / an*.

annoyed   cold   ~~disappointing~~   expensive   disappointed   long   rude

Liz: Hi Alice. Have you been to that new café in town yet? What was it like?

Alice: It wasn't great. It was ¹*rather a disappointing* experience.

Liz: I'm surprised! My brother's been and he thought that their cakes were delicious – although
²_____. He said nothing cost less than $4! What happened?

Alice: Well, it was very busy and we had to wait ³_____ time to get served. A big group of people arrived about ten minutes after we sat down and the waiter ignored us and served them first. We felt ⁴_____ about that.

Liz: Yes, I hate it when that happens.

Alice: And the waiter, when he finally served us, was ⁵_____ man. He didn't say sorry when he brought us the wrong cakes; he just looked angry when we tried to tell him they weren't what we had ordered. When he brought us the right cakes, they were extremely small and Mum's coffee was ⁶_____, so, all in all, we were ⁷_____.

Use of English: present perfect with time expressions

SB p.77

1 **Match the beginnings (1–6) and the endings (a–f) to make sentences.**

1 He's already chopped up the vegetables   _d_
2 I can't believe that you still haven't finished chopping the vegetables –   _____
3 She's only chopped about half the carrots so far,   _____
4 We've just finished chopping the vegetables   _____
5 I don't think I've bought any more carrots recently   _____
6 They haven't even started chopping the vegetables yet –   _____

a they're still washing their hands and getting ready.
b and she hasn't even started on the other vegetables.
c and I'm worried there won't be enough for the soup.
d ~~and put them in the soup.~~
e so we're going to start making the soup.
f can't you work any faster?

2 Complete the second sentence so it means the same as the first sentence. Use the adverbs in brackets.

1 There's a new restaurant in town, but we still haven't been to it. (yet)
We haven't *been to the new restaurant in town yet*.

2 The last time I ate chicken was a few months ago. (recently)
I haven't _____

3 It's been a long time since they did any cooking. (for ages)
They haven't _____

4 I know this isn't the first time I've drunk watermelon juice. (in the past)
I'm sure I've _____

5 It's been a long time since I saw olives like these in the market. (for a while)
I haven't _____

6 I've never eaten such a delicious curry. (in my life)
It's the most _____

Vocabulary: adjectives for describing food

SB p.78

Complete the sentences with the words from the box.

| sour | creamy | crispy | ~~fresh~~ | juicy | salty | spicy | sweet |

1 I love *fresh* food: the more recently something has been taken out of the ground or the sea, the better!

2 The watermelon was so _____ that we had to dry our hands and faces after eating it.

3 Unfortunately, I love cake, biscuits, chocolates and anything _____, although I try not to eat too many of them.

4 I also enjoy _____ snacks like crisps and peanuts, though they make me very thirsty.

5 My best friend is Indian and I love the hot, _____ dishes her mother makes.

6 He loves to eat lemons; he likes the strong, _____ taste.

7 For breakfast, my brother likes a nice, _____ cereal that makes a loud noise as you eat it.

8 If I've been ill, I like soft, _____ foods like yoghurt and ice cream that don't hurt your throat.

Vocabulary: food and cooking

Read the clues and complete the crossword. The words are all connected to food.

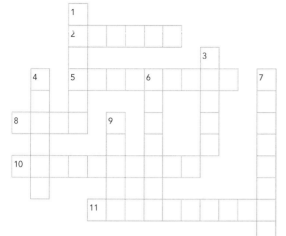

Across

2 A juicy fruit that is also the name of a colour.

5 We use this adjective to say something tastes good.

8 A very popular food in Asia. It comes from a plant, it's white and sushi is made with it.

10 This is a place where we pay to sit and eat food that somebody else has prepared.

11 We use this adjective to describe a dish that doesn't have meat in it.

Down

1 A type of pasta that is used a lot in Japanese and Chinese cooking.

3 A spicy dish from India which can be made with vegetables or meat.

4 These small fruits are usually green or black. You often find them on top of pizzas.

6 This large round, green vegetable is served raw in salads, or cooked or made into soup.

7 A small ball of dough (= flour and water) that is cooked and eaten with meat or vegetables.

9 A liquid or paste that is served with a dish to make it taste more interesting.

Check your progress

1 What can you do now?

I can …

talk and write about food ☐

make comparisons with *not only / also* and *neither / nor* ☐

use different adverbs with the present perfect ☐

understand an internet show about food and restaurants ☐

write a description of a delicious dish ☐

2 Answer the questions about this unit.

1 What have you enjoyed most?

_____

2 Is there anything you have found difficult?

_____

3 What would you like to learn more about?

_____

My learning

What did you learn in this unit?

Vocabulary: my style
SB p.84

Read the text again. Then find the words in the wordsearch to complete the sentences (1–8).

1 F<u>unctional</u> clothes protect your body and keep you warm but nothing more.

2 A look that is very fashionable and absolutely the latest style is b_____ _____ _____.

3 S_____ clothes are for when you need to look good in formal situations.

4 C_____ clothes are things like jeans that you wear to feel relaxed and comfortable.

5 You know you are c_____ when people want to look like you and copy your style.

6 Children usually like bright, **c**_____ clothes.

7 C_____ clothes are in styles that don't change with time and are always popular.

8 Active people often like to wear **s**_____ clothes such as running shorts and trainers.

f	u	n	c	t	i	o	n	a	l	k	o
b	n	s	r	o	r	t	e	r	o	e	r
z	c	o	l	o	u	r	f	u	l	a	s
c	o	p	r	a	i	s	g	t	w	u	t
l	b	a	n	g	o	n	t	r	e	n	d
a	s	n	a	i	r	w	k	i	n	c	a
s	m	g	c	a	s	u	a	l	n	o	n
s	a	i	x	i	n	g	o	r	q	o	s
i	r	s	s	p	o	r	t	y	u	l	i
c	t	e	c	l	o	a	c	k	e	a	r

Reading: comprehension
SB p.85

Read the text again and choose the best words or phrases to complete the sentences.

1 American teenagers are spending more [more / less] on clothes and [more / less] on food and the internet than they did in the past.

2 The most important status symbol for teenagers these days is [a pair of designer trainers / an up-to-date smartphone or tablet].

3 Instead of shopping for clothes, teenagers are spending time [eating in cafés / surfing the internet in cafés].

4 It's possible that teenagers today spend less money because [they are more responsible than in the past / the economy has not been as good as in the past].

5 Because of this, many fashion shops for teenagers have closed or now only sell clothes [online / in markets].

Reading: thinking about the text

SB p.85

Answer the questions.

1 According to the article, how have teenagers' interests and habits changed since 2003?

_____

_____

_____

2 You want to start a business selling clothes to teenagers. Write three sentences about how you will make sure each of these things attracts teenagers:

Price: _____

Styles: _____

Marketing and selling: _____

Vocabulary: words in context

SB p.86

Read this conversation between Marc, who wants to start a fashion business, and Laura, a teenager who loves fashion. Complete it with the words from the box.

browsing	develop	designer	effect	generation
global recession		marketing strategy		status symbol

Marc: How important are clothes and fashion to you and your ¹_____?

Laura: Most of us think they are very important. But not everyone my age would agree. I love clothes, especially ²_____ clothes. I love Nike and Levi.

Marc: So are stylish clothes a ³_____ for you and your friends?

Laura: Yes, definitely. I believe that the way you dress has an ⁴_____ on how people think about you.

Marc: So, do you spend a lot of time clothes shopping?

Laura: Yes. Shopping is one of my favourite hobbies. But I spend much more time ⁵_____ than buying. I look and look but I don't always buy.

Marc: Lots of fashion companies have had to close shops recently because of the ⁶_____. Their new ⁷_____ is to advertise and sell their clothes online. Do you think you spend more time shopping online?

Laura: I do spend a lot of time online, but I still love going into real shops and seeing and touching things. I think clothes companies should ⁸_____ their online shopping but they shouldn't forget about real shops.

Vocabulary: compound adjectives

SB p.86

Complete the advertising descriptions with the adjectives from the boxes. There is one in each box that you do not need.

| cutting-edge | multi-coloured | ultra-light | extra-large |

1 Our new summer beach-bag is made of _____ material and weighs almost nothing. Bring all you need for a day by the sea!

2 The new Experian 6 laptop is one of the most advanced on the market today. Enjoy showing your friends its _____ features.

3 Little girls will love this bright, _____ sundress.

| eye-catching | extra-strong | up-to-date | multi-coloured |

4 The YCX phone has all the latest and most _____ features for texting, calling and surfing the net, so staying in contact with your friends will be quicker and easier.

5 People will notice you on the beach this summer in our _____ black-and-white sunhat. It's not only stylish but also practical, helping you stay cool in the heat.

6 Stay out of the rain this spring with our smart new umbrellas. Made from special _____ material, they will keep you safe and dry even in stormy weather.

Use of English: present perfect passive

SB p.86

Rewrite the sentences using the present perfect passive.

1 "The global recession has affected us badly," say big fashion companies.
Big fashion companies have been badly _affected by the global recession_.

2 Instagram has replaced TV and magazines as the place where teenagers learn about fashion.
TV and magazines _____.

3 We have completely repainted the inside of the shop.
The inside of the shop _____.

4 We have changed our look to something brighter and more modern.
Our look _____.

5 The company has employed a team of new designers.

_____

6 We have developed an online marketing strategy.

_____

Vocabulary: words in context

SB p.88

Complete the sentences with the words and phrases from the box.

bullies	gender-neutral	human rights	identity	potential	pressure

1 The _____ problem of students worrying about how they look is reduced if everyone wears the same thing.

2 In a _____ environment, boys and girls follow exactly the same rules.

3 Being free to make choices and being allowed to look how you want are _____.

4 _____ often make fun of students who look a bit different from other people.

5 The way you dress can be a way of showing your _____ to the world.

6 Teenagers sometimes feel that they are under a lot of _____ to look good.

Use of English: modal verbs

SB p.88

Choose the best option to complete the text.

Hi Olivia,

It was great to hear about English school life. Our school day here is from about 7:30 to 1:30, although these times ^{1}__ exactly the same everywhere. In my school, for example, we start at 7:15 a.m. You ^{2}__ late, not even by one minute. If you do, you ^{3}__ or even sent home. Another thing that is different is that we all ^{4}__ exercise in the morning – judo, karate or yoga. I chose judo this year but I'm not very good at it. I ^{5}__ to do yoga next year if I can.

I was interested to hear that in England you ^{6}__ up when the teacher comes into the classroom. We do! We call our teachers "Ma'am" and "Sir" and the whole class ^{7}__ silent when they are speaking.

I must go now – I've got lots of homework this evening.

Write soon!

Kavita

1 a mustn't be   b may not be   c must be   d might be

2 a don't have to arrive   b mustn't arrive   c might not arrive   d must arrive

3 a must be punished   b might not be punished
  c may be punished   d may not be punished

4 a have to do   b has to do   c must to do   d don't have to do

5 a can change   b have to change   c might change   d don't have to change

6 a can stand   b don't have to stand   c might stand   d have to stand

7 a mustn't be   b can be   c doesn't have to be   d must be

Vocabulary: multiword verbs with *pick*

1 Look again at this sentence from the listening text and choose the correct meaning (a–c) for pick on.

We mustn't forget that school uniform gives potential bullies one less thing to <u>pick on</u> as well.

a be kind to someone   b be unkind to someone, over and over again   c ignore someone

2 Match the meaning of pick + preposition in these sentences with the correct definitions (a–d).

1 I'll <u>pick</u> you <u>up</u> at 3'clock.
2 He <u>picked out</u> his favourite shirt to wear.
3 Sam <u>picked up</u> the suitcases of clothes.
4 We don't speak much Spanish, but we'll <u>pick</u> it <u>up</u> when we get there.

a choose something from a group of things
b lift something up
c learn from experience
d collect someone, often in a car

3 Complete the sentences with the verbs from the box. You can use each verb more than once and you may have to change the form.

> pick on   pick out   pick up

1 Could you _____ me _____ from the station at 4:30?

2 Can you _____ which animal doesn't live in the sea?

3 Nobody taught him to play the guitar, he just _____ it _____.

4 Please _____ that piece of rubbish and put it in the bin.

5 They _____ him at school because he was so shy.

Check your progress

1 What can you do now?

I can …

understand and discuss an article about teenage fashion ☐

talk about style and fashion choices and school uniform ☐

💡 My learning
What did you learn in this unit?

use the present perfect passive ☐

understand and use modals of possibility and obligation ☐

write an opinion essay ☐

2 Answer the questions about this unit.

1 What have you enjoyed most?

_____

2 Is there anything you have found difficult?

_____

3 What would you like to learn more about?

Mid-year review

Vocabulary: word hunt

Can you remember four words you have learned that are:

Unit 1: adjectives for describing personality

Unit 2: verbs for important life events

Unit 3: nouns for rooms and furniture

Unit 4: compound nouns related to transport

Unit 5: advantages and disadvantages of tourism

Unit 6: nouns to describe our senses

Unit 7: adjectives for describing food

Unit 8: adjectives for describing style / fashion

Vocabulary: a crossword puzzle

Read the clues and complete the crossword.

Across

2 A **p**_____ is an amount of something, e.g. of food that you are served in restaurant.

5 A **s**_____ **s**_____ is an object a person has which shows how rich, cool or important he / she is.

6 **S**_____ is visiting places that are interesting because they are historical or famous.

8 All the people in your family are your **r**_____.

9 A group of people who live together in the same place is a **c**_____.

10 **B**_____ is looking at things in shops but not buying anything.

Down

1 The things that belong to you are your **p**_____.

3 You are **o**_____ when you are connected to the internet.

4 You have to type in your **p**_____ to open your computer or see your social media sites.

7 When people get married, they have a **w**_____.

Use of English: correction competition

Correct two mistakes in each sentence or pair of sentences. Tick (✓) the mistakes as you find them.

- full stop missing at the end of the sentence ☐
- missing comma ☑ ☐ ☐
- missing capital letter/s ☑ ☐ ☐
- missing question mark ☐
- missing apostrophe ☐ ☐ ☐
- spelling mistake ☐ ☐ ☐

1 I've just started studying *G*german, and I already speak English French and Spanish.

2 generally speaking, I enjoy school however I'm not the most academic person in the world.

3 I love looking after my neices and nephews. I want to work with children when I'm older

4 Id like to study in an English-speaking country. Do you think that would be a good idea.

5 He's the cleverest most popular boy in our class and he's going to study in the usa next year.

6 Its true that I can be a bit lazy sometimes, but that's usualy only when I'm bored by something.

7 My sisters best freind is going to move to a different school and my sister is very upset about it.

Quiz: *Focus on ...*

Can you remember these things from the Focus on ... sections in the Student's Book?

1 A type of technology that helps light to travel anywhere very fast. _____
_____

2 The city in South Africa where Mzal' uJola comes to live. _____

3 The names of these three-dimensional shapes.

_____ _____ _____ _____

4 The name and location of the world's oldest underground train system.
_____ _____

5 A form of tourism which aims not to damage the environment. _____

6 The first thing Miss Honey asked Matilda to do in front of the class. _____

7 The word for a picture of a place made out of food. _____

8 What the word *sombrero* means in English. _____

The great outdoors

Reading: comprehension
SB p.100

Read the text again and decide if the sentences are true or false or it doesn't say. Correct the false sentences.

1 Scientists have proved that spending time outside is good for you.

True / False / Doesn't say

2 The colour green is very popular with cyclists.

True / False / Doesn't say

3 Going outside for two minutes wakes you up more than a cup of coffee.

True / False / Doesn't say

4 Spending time in the sunshine helps to develop healthy bones.

True / False / Doesn't say

5 People's hearts beat faster after spending time outside.

True / False / Doesn't say

6 Being in a beautiful natural setting can cure illness.

True / False / Doesn't say

Reading: thinking about the text
SB pp. 100–101

How can spending time outside:

1 help your body?

_____

_____

2 help the way you feel?

_____

_____

Vocabulary: words in context
SB p.101

Complete the sentences with the words from the box.

| creativity | depression | mood | proof | relaxation |

1 _____ is difficult for many teenagers: they don't find it easy to forget their worries and do nothing.

2 Your _____, the way that you feel, is controlled by your mind and also by your body if it is cold, hungry, tired, and so on.

3 If you often feel sad and tired for no special reason, you may have _____.

4 Artists and writers have higher levels of _____ than most people.

5 You will have to give me some _____ if you want me to believe this is true.

Use of English: conjunctions

1 Match the conjunctions in these sentences from the text with other conjunctions with similar meanings (a–d) below.

1 A group of cyclists who were in front of some green pictures found exercise easier **whereas** another group who were in front of grey and red pictures found it harder.

2 Do you find it hard to start the day **unless** you've had a cup of coffee?

3 Most of us don't get enough Vitamin D in our diets, **except** those who take vitamin pills.

4 Scientists have found that people's hearts start to beat more slowly **once** they have been outside for a while.

a when

b apart from

c but

d if not

2 Rewrite the sentences. Use the conjunction in brackets.

1 I didn't enjoy hiking at first because I used to feel so tired. (once)

Once I stopped feeling so tired, I enjoyed hiking.

2 I'm afraid you can't come with us if you don't bring your own picnic. (unless)

_____ your own picnic, I'm afraid you can't come with us.

3 She used to spend all her time hiking, but now she says she hates the countryside. (whereas)

Now she says _____

4 Most of the time I love camping, but I don't enjoy it when it's raining. (except)

I love _____

5 After I had fallen into the water a few times, I stopped being afraid of it. (once)

_____ a few times, I stopped being afraid of it.

6 We need to walk a bit faster or we'll never get home before it's dark. (unless)

_____

we'll never get home before it's dark.

3 Complete the sentences (a–d) using your own ideas.

a I like to go cycling in the forest whereas …

b Everyone likes camping except …

c Sarah won't go hiking unless …

d People usually enjoy swimming once …

Vocabulary: camping

SB p.102

Complete the text with the words from the box.

| canoe | creative | hike | shelter | skills | tent |

I'm going to a survival camp next week – I can't wait! We are going on a long [1]_____ in the mountains and we have to carry everything we need. We aren't even taking a [2]_____ to sleep in. We have to build our own [3]_____ from natural materials. Our teacher says we will need to be [4]_____ and learn to use what is around us. I'm going to learn lots of other [5]_____ as well, like how to make a fire and cook on it. We're also going to travel down a river by [6]_____. I've never been in a boat before so I'm really excited!

Vocabulary: nouns that are both countable and uncountable

SB p.102

Complete the pairs of sentences with a noun from the box. Use the correct countable and uncountable form.

| hair | memory | sport | time |

1 I've never been good at _____ and I'm not at all interested in it.

Tennis, hockey and athletics are examples of different _____.

2 My sister has long, blonde _____.

I've just found two black _____ in the butter and I want to know where they came from.

3 We have happy _____ of our childhood.

My grandfather is very old and he is starting to lose his _____.

4 _____ passes very slowly when you are bored and have nothing to do.

I've seen this film three _____ already.

Vocabulary: idioms

SB p.104

Replace the underlined part of each sentence with an idiom from the box.

| find your feet | jumped out of my skin | like a fish out of water | thrown in at the deep end |

1 When I first started my new school I felt that I didn't belong there at all.

I felt _____.

2 Living away from home will be difficult at first but I'm sure you will soon be able to manage very well.

I'm sure you will soon _____.

3 I'd never looked after small children before, so when I was left with four small boys I was made to do something I wasn't ready to do and didn't have the skills for.

I was _____.

4 I hadn't heard him come into the room, so when he touched my shoulder, I was very surprised and frightened.

I nearly _____.

Use of English: *have / get* something done

SB p.104

Complete the sentences. Use the words in brackets.

1 The living room was looking a bit dark and dirty so we _____.
   (get / repaint)

2 He didn't want us to come with him so we _____. (let / go alone)

3 My father told my brother his hair was much too long so he _____.
   (make / get a haircut)

4 The kitchen window got broken so we _____. (have / replace)

5 The children were tired so their parents _____.
   (make / to bed early)

6 We told the sports teacher our legs were aching and he _____!
   (let / stop / rest)

Use of English: modals – *must have, can't have*

SB p.105

Write sentences with *must have* or *can't have* and the words in brackets. You will need to change the verb form.

1 I was sure I brought my red jumper with me but I can't find it in my backpack.

   I _____.
   (forget it)

2 I left a note on her desk asking her to ring me but she never called.

   She _____.
   (see my message)

3 "When I got off the plane I had been travelling for 24 hours."

   "You _____."
   (be very tired)

4 "I waved and smiled at him but he didn't wave back."

   "He _____." (recognise you)

5 I don't know where they are but their bags and coats are still here.

   They _____. (leave the building)

6 I thought there was some cake left, but when I looked in the cupboard, it was empty.

   The children _____. (eat it)

Vocabulary: physical education

Read the clues and complete the crossword.

Across

3 _____ is the ability to move about quickly and easily.

6 Sportspeople are always trying to improve their _____ in their individual sport.

7 He has great _____ and can run long distances without stopping or getting tired.

8 I work out with weights to try to get bigger _____ in my arms.

Down

1 Tennis players try to make their arms stronger so they can increase their _____ to hit the ball harder.

2 An _____ is someone who is good at sports and physical exercise.

4 He can run at a _____ of almost 15 kilometres per hour!

5 When you start riding a bicycle, you have to learn to keep your _____ and not fall off.

Check your progress

1 What can you do now?

I can …

understand an article about spending time outdoors ☐	use a range of conjunctions in speech and writing ☐
talk about outdoor activities and survival camps ☐	understand and use *have / get* something done ☐

My learning

What did you learn in this unit?

2 Answer the questions about this unit.

1 What have you enjoyed most?

_____

2 Is there anything you have found difficult?

_____

3 What would you like to learn more about?

_____

10 Treasure!

Reading: comprehension
SB pp.110–111

1 **Read the text again and decide if the sentences are true or false.**

1 People almost never find treasure any more. There is none left to find.   True / False

2 In 2009, a British man found treasure in a field using a metal detector.   True / False

3 Hidden boxes of gold and silver coins were found by builders in Nepal.   True / False

4 The five boxes of treasure had been hidden in a store room for 300 years.   True / False

5 A 16-year-old girl found a big piece of gold in lake in a Germany in 2015.   True / False

6 Forrest Fenn drew a map to show where he hid his treasure.   True / False

2 **Now correct the false sentences.**

_____

_____

_____

Reading: thinking about the text
SB p.111

Answer the questions.

1 Which of the discoveries do you think is the most exciting? Why?

_____

_____

2 Would you like to look for Forest Fenn's treasure? Why? Why not?

_____

_____

Vocabulary: words in context

SB p.111

Complete the article with the words from the box. You may have to change the form of some words.

| worth | chest | discovery | hunt | jewel | valuable | weigh |

Amazing treasure under the streets of London

Builders working on the London underground have made an amazing
[1] _____.

Three big [2] _____ full of treasure have been found hidden less than a metre away from a major underground train station, where trains pass every day.

The treasure is extremely [3] _____ and is [4] _____ at least 10 million

dollars. It includes pieces of gold, some of which [5] _____ as much as half a kilo. There are also [6] _____ of different sizes – some of them are in rings and bracelets and some are separate stones.

Archaeologists [7] _____ for more information about where the treasure came from, but only have 48 hours before the station will open to trains again.

Vocabulary: multiword verbs with come

SB p.112

Complete the sentences with the multiword verbs from the box. You may have to change the form of the verbs.

| come across | come down | come up | come on | come out | come forward |

1 I _____ this article by accident when I was looking for something else.

2 A film about the Kathmandu treasure has just _____ and it's on at the cinema.

3 If we hurry up we can get tickets. _____! Let's get the bus into town.

4 We were talking about clever people and your name _____ in the conversation!

5 The police are waiting for someone who saw the accident to _____.

6 The price has _____ a little recently but silver will always be valuable.

Use of English: spelling

SB p.112

Find and correct six spelling mistakes.

"What are those people doing in that feild?" I asked.

"There using a metal detector to look for treasure," answered my dad.

"But surely their isn't any treasure here!" I said. "It's just ordinary countryside."

"Recently people have found peaces of gold and silver coins on the hillside using they're metal detectors," said dad. "They think there is more treasure under the hill, and they won't leave us in piece until they have found it."

Vocabulary: geocaching

SB p.113

1 Match the words in the box with their meanings (a–d). Use a dictionary, if necessary.

> compass   location   logbook   satellite

a a piece of equipment that is sent into space around the Earth to receive and send signals or to collect information

b a notebook in which people write information that can be checked by someone else

c a piece of equipment that people use to find which way north is

d a place or position

2 Complete the dialogue with the words from the box.

> compass   location   logbook   map   satellites   SatNav

Jim: Can you explain how geocaching works? I don't understand what a GPS is or how it helps you find the treasure.

Axel: OK. Well, GPS stands for global position system. There is a group of ¹_____ in space that are moving round the Earth. If you have a GPS receiver (which is a small machine you hold in your hand), this communicates with the GPS system and can give you your exact ²_____ anywhere on the Earth! When I go geocaching with my dad I use a ³_____ This receives the information from the GPS system and shows you where you are on a ⁴_____.

Jim: So I guess you don't even need to use a ⁵_____ to show you where north is – that's amazing! So what kind of treasure can you find?

Axel: The treasure itself isn't usually very exciting or valuable. It's a collection of items – such as coins and plastic figures – in a small box. Inside the box, there's also a ⁶_____ where you write your name and the date you found the treasure.

Use of English: reported speech

SB p.114

1 Write what the teacher said to the children on the school trip as reported speech.

1 "Listen carefully, children, and do exactly what I say."

The teacher told the children to listen carefully and do exactly what he said.

2 "Don't forget your things when you get off the bus."

He told us not _____.

3 "Your parents have paid for your visit to the museum."

He told us that _____.

4 "You will need to take money for drinks and snacks."

He said _____.

2 Write the questions the children asked as reported speech.

1 Paul: "When are we going to have lunch?"

Paul asked when they were going to have lunch.

2 Arabella: "Can I go to the museum shop?"

_____

3 Louise: "Where can I fill my water bottle?"

_____

4 Robin: "Is there a place to buy drinks?"

_____

Use of English: understanding and being understood | SB p.114

1 Put the words in the correct order to make phrases we can use to help us understand, and to check we have been understood.

a before Year 1. / means / So, in other words, / BCE

So, in other words, BCE means before Year 1.

b you said? / the first thing / repeat / Could you

_____

c what / don't / I still / you mean. / understand

_____

d you. / I don't / I'm afraid / follow

_____

2 Complete the conversation with phrases a–d from Activity 1 above.

Teacher: So the treasure is very old because it dates from 700BCE, or before common era.

Student: Sorry, but ¹*d* Could you say that again?

Teacher: BCE stands for "before common era".

Student: I'm sorry, ²___ What does "before common era" mean? What is the common era?

Teacher: The "common era" is the period since we started counting years in our calendar from Year 1. ³___

Student: OK. ⁴___

Teacher: The treasure is very old because it dates from 700BCE.

Vocabulary: treasure

Find the words in the wordsearch to complete the sentences.

h	i	r	s	h	t	u	b	l	u	c
i	y	u	m	u	s	e	u	m	s	o
d	e	t	e	c	t	o	r	f	h	i
d	r	i	s	g	e	n	i	l	o	n
e	s	p	i	r	a	t	e	s	r	s
n	t	g	n	n	i	m	d	t	y	x
t	o	o	u	z	c	k	o	e	a	o
r	p	l	w	s	i	l	v	e	r	o
a	e	d	g	g	h	a	e	m	a	p

1 It's not easy to find treasure because it is usually **h**_idden_.

2 Some people have found treasure using a metal **d**_____.

3 Treasure is often **b**_____ in the ground.

4 If you are lucky, you might have a **m**_____ which shows you where the treasure is.

5 **P**_____ are often interested in treasure and steal it when they can.

6 **M**_____ are places where ordinary people can go to look at and enjoy famous treasures.

7 Treasure usually contains objects made of **g**_____, a beautiful and expensive yellow metal.

8 **S**_____ is another beautiful, shiny metal: it is often used to make rings and bracelets.

9 **C**_____ are round metal objects used as money.

Check your progress

1 **What can you do now?**

I can ...

talk and write about treasure ☐

spell words which sound the same correctly ☐

understand a radio programme about geocaching ☐

use reported speech ☐

ask for help when I haven't understood ☐

💡 **My learning**
What did you learn in this unit?

2 **Answer the questions about this unit.**

1 What have you enjoyed most?

_____

2 Is there anything you have found difficult?

_____

3 What would you like to learn more about?

_____

Reading: comprehension

SB p.122

Read the text again and complete the sentences with one word.

1 Jake Nickell made his hobby into a successful _____.

2 His company, which makes T-shirts, is called _____.

3 He got the idea for starting his company after he won an online _____.

4 He was disappointed that he didn't get to see his winning _____ printed on a T-shirt.

5 Jake now uses _____ to get ideas for what to put on his T-shirts.

6 There are about two _____ people in Jake's online community.

7 He gets thousands of ideas for T-shirts every month but only chooses about _____.

8 People sometimes play _____ during important meetings in Jake's company.

Reading: thinking about the text

SB p.122

Read the text again and answer the questions.

1 In what ways is Jake's company different and unusual?

_____

_____

2 Why do you think he gets so many ideas for T-shirts from people online?

_____

_____

3 What would you like to have as a design on a T-shirt?

_____

_____

Vocabulary: words in context

SB p.123

Complete the sentences with the words from the box.

creative	community	designers	profit	submit	vote

1 We didn't spend much on materials and we've sold for a good price: we're going to make a _____ this year.

2 I think the group should _____ for the idea we like best.

3 There is a _____ of people who are interested in this project and we exchange ideas and comments online.

4 She is an extremely _____ artist who is always full of new ideas.

5 "How shall we _____ our ideas?" "You can describe them in writing or send photos."

6 It's our _____ who think of the ideas and decide how the T-shirt is going to look.

Vocabulary: word building

SB p.123

1 Complete the table. Use a dictionary, if necessary. All these words (but not all the forms) are from the text on page 122 of the Student's Book.

Adjective	Noun	Verb
1 _____	creativity	2 _____
3 _____	success	4 _____
5 _____	disappointment	disappoint

2 Complete the dialogue with words from the table in Activity 1 above. You may have to change the form of some words.

Interviewer: Frank, well done for winning 'Young Entrepreneur of the Year'. Can you share with us some of the secrets of your ¹s_____?

Frank: First of all, I want to say that my business wasn't ²s_____ immediately. At the beginning, I made a lot of mistakes and had a lot of ³d_____.

Interviewer: Can you give us an example?

Frank: I was extremely ⁴d_____ when the business didn't make a profit in its first year! But then I realised that I needed to lower my prices.

Interviewer: So, did you do that?

Frank: Yes, I did it immediately. You need to make up your mind to do things quickly in business. You also have to keep having new ideas! ⁵C_____ is very important.

Use of English: adding interest to sentences

SB p.124

Rewrite the sentences (1–6). Add more detail to the underlined nouns to make longer noun phrases. You can use:

- adjectives (*the tall, dark man*)
- relative clauses (*the man who we met last year*)
- phrases with prepositions (*the man on the train*)
- adjective and adverbs (*the extremely good-looking and remarkably talented man*)

1 The young <u>man</u> set up an <u>internet business</u>.

   The tall, blond young man who I met in Germany set up an unusual internet business.

2 This <u>designer</u> gave us the ideas for our <u>website</u>.

   _____

3 She was an <u>entrepreneur</u> who set up her own <u>jewellery business</u>.

   _____

4 The <u>women</u> started to sell their <u>cakes</u> in the <u>market</u>.

   _____

5 The <u>waiter</u> took the <u>plates</u> off the <u>table</u>.

   _____

6 The <u>woman</u> drove the <u>car</u> through the <u>forest</u>.

   _____

Use of English: compound nouns

SB p.124

Make three compound nouns with nouns 1–6 below. Use the words in the box to help you. You can use each word more than once. Use a dictionary to check if the compound nouns are written as one or two words.

basket	bed	board	college	competition	conference	costume	dining	foot
gallery	game	hand	man	paper	park	plastic	pool	racing	student	sports	suit

1 For example: ball   *basketball   football   ball game*

2 business   _____   _____   _____

3 art   _____   _____   _____

4 room   _____   _____   _____

5 bag   _____   _____   _____

6 car   _____   _____   _____

7 swimming   _____   _____   _____

Use of English: past modals

1 Choose the best options (a–c) to complete the email.

Hi Sami

I'm helping my friend with her teashop business this summer. I ¹___ to the beach with my family, but I decided not to because Sonia doesn't have enough people to help her. I told her she ²___ a dishwasher but she said she didn't have the money to buy one when she started the business. She hadn't planned to open this summer but a shop became free and she knew she had to take it. The place ³___ available a month later. I think she made a good decision and she ⁴___ at a better time because right now there is a summer arts festival so the town is full of tourists. But she ⁵___ so much money on painting and decorating the shop. It's bright pink and I think it looks terrible!

Tamara

1 a couldn't have gone	**b** could have gone	**c** must have gone
2 a should have bought	**b** must have bought	**c** might have bought
3 a couldn't have been	**b** shouldn't have been	**c** mightn't have been
4 a shouldn't have started	**b** couldn't have started	**c** could have started
5 a mightn't have spent	**b** shouldn't have spent	**c** couldn't have spent

2 Complete the sentences with *could(n't) have*, *should(n't) have*, or *might(n't) have*. Sometimes more than one answer is possible.

1 "Do you know where your school bag is?" "I've looked everywhere but I just can't find it. I <u>*might have / could have*</u> left it on the bus."

2 It wasn't a good idea to pay for all those posters. We _____ spent so much on advertising.

3 It was silly of me to want to do everything by myself. I _____ asked my parents for help.

4 I can't see his car outside so he _____ arrived yet.

5 Her parents gave her good advice. She _____ listened to it.

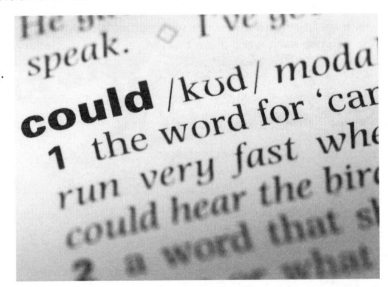

6 It _____ been my brother that you saw last night. He's in Australia at the moment.

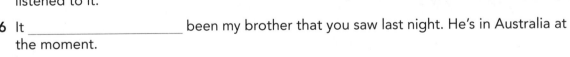

Vocabulary: the Silk Roads

SB p.128

Read the clues and complete the crossword.

Across

4 The Silk Roads began at the time when the Han D_____ ruled China.

7 There was a lot of cultural e_____ amongst the travellers on the Silk Roads.

9 The Silk Roads affected how different c_____ developed.

Down

1 Because of the Silk Roads, people from different c_____s started meeting each other.

2 The t_____s along the Silk Roads bought and sold many different sorts of products.

3 Rich people from the West wanted to buy c_____ from China to make fine clothes.

5 T_____ on the Silk Roads was usually by camel or by horse; it was slow and difficult.

6 The Silk Roads had a big i_____ on the history of all the countries it passed through.

8 The Chinese were the only people who knew how to make s_____.

Check your progress

1 What can you do now?

I can ...

talk and write about entrepreneurs ☐

use compound nouns and noun phrases ☐

understand a radio programme about teenage entrepreneurs ☐

2 Answer the questions about this unit.

1 What have you enjoyed most?

_____

2 Is there anything you have found difficult?

_____

3 What would you like to learn more about?

_____

 My learning

What did you learn in this unit?

understand and use past modals ☐

give a presentation about a business idea ☐

12 Sleep

Vocabulary: sleep habits

SB p.132

Complete the text with the words from the box.

bedtime	exhausted	lack	nightmares	pillow
	questionnaire	switch off	tiredness	

Our class has been working on a [1]_____ about our sleep habits. We have found that a [2]_____ of sleep is a big problem for many of us. Many teenagers suffer from [3]_____. Because we are still growing and developing, we need enough rest or we can quickly become [4]_____ and get ill. We found out that it is important to [5]_____ our mobile phones and computers at least one hour before our head hits the [6]_____. It is also true that watching a sad or frightening film or video before you sleep can give you [7]_____. The best thing we can do before [8]_____ is an activity many of us find difficult: just relax!

Use of English: adverbs

SB p.133

1 Read the Language tip. Then match the types of adverb (1–6) with the examples (a–e).

> **Language tip**
> **Adverbs** can be used with a verb, adjective or another adverb. They add information about *how, how often, how much, where* and *when* something happens, and how certain we feel about it.

Types of adverb
1 adverbs of manner (how something happens)
2 adverbs of frequency (how often something happens)
3 adverbs of degree (how much / to what extent something happens)
4 adverbs of place (where something happens)
5 adverbs of time (when something happens)
6 adverbs of certainty (how sure / certain we are about something happening)

Examples
a *often, rarely, never, seldom, once a week* (for example, He rarely gets to bed before ten.)
b *upstairs, everywhere, inside, over there, above* (for example, They went upstairs to bed.)
c *probably, definitely, possibly, certainly, undoubtedly* (for example, He probably needs to get more sleep.)
d *slowly, badly, carefully, happily, fast* (for example, I slept badly last night.)
e *very, quite, extremely, completely, really, nearly* (for example, It's extremely difficult to sleep in this heat.)
f *later, afterwards, earlier, previously, yesterday* (for example, We watched TV and went to bed later.)

2 Complete the answers to the questions with the best adverb(s) from the box.

> ~~definitely~~   extremely   carefully   once or twice
> upstairs, above the kitchen

1 How sure are you that Camille should get more sleep?
   Camille should _definitely_ get more sleep.
2 How often do you wake up in the night?
   I wake up _____ in the night.
3 How did they study the results of the sleep questionnaire?
   They studied the results of the sleep questionnaire _____.
4 Where does he sleep?
   He sleeps _____.
5 How difficult is it to understand the information?
   The information is _____ difficult to understand.

Reading: comprehension SB p.134

Read the four texts on page 134 of the Student's Book about sleep again. Decide if the sentences are true, false or it doesn't say. Correct the sentences that are false.

1 A lack of sleep can make you feel angry.   True / False / Doesn't say
2 Reading in bed can stop you from going to sleep.   True / False / Doesn't say
3 Getting enough sleep is good for your skin.   True / False / Doesn't say
4 The traveller in Siberia was amazed by sleeping bears.   True / False / Doesn't say
5 The writer of text C has probably developed
   sleeping problems because of worrying a lot.   True / False / Doesn't say
6 Randy Gardner can live without sleep for more than
   11 days without feeling tired.   True / False / Doesn't say

Reading: thinking about the text SB p.134

1 Which of the four texts in the Student's Book gives the most information about the importance of sleep? How does it do this? (You can compare it to the other three.)

_____

_____

2 What advice would you offer the writer of the letter in text C if you were Angie?

_____

_____

Vocabulary: words in context

SB p.135

Complete the sentences with the words from the box. You may have to change the form of some words.

anxious   concentrate   experiment   hibernate   peacefully   stressed

1 I hate the cold weather and the long, dark evenings, so I think that going to sleep
   and _____ all winter is a very good idea!

2 There have been many scientific _____ to find out about the effects of lack of
   sleep on humans.

3 Small children are able to sleep _____ at night because they don't have any
   worries or problems in their lives.

4 He got very _____ by the noise the other students were making when he was
   trying to study.

5 I don't find it very easy to _____ on what I'm doing if I haven't had
   enough sleep.

6 My teacher noticed I was looking unhappy and asked me what I was _____
   about.

Use of English: adjective + preposition

SB p.135

Complete the second sentence so that it has a similar meaning to the first sentence.
Use no more than *three* words.

1 She doesn't want to stay up late because she is afraid she will feel tired
   the next morning.

   She doesn't want to stay up late because she is *afraid of feeling* tired the
   next morning.

2 My new bedroom is similar to my old one.

   My new bedroom isn't very
   _____ the one I had before.

3 Because my father didn't sleep on the
   plane, he is anxious that he might fall
   asleep while driving.

   My father didn't sleep on the plane so he
   is _____ asleep while
   driving.

4 He won't fail the exam – tell him not to
   worry about it!

   Tell him not to _____
   the exam.

Reading: a dream story

SB p.137

Match the beginnings of the sentences (1–7) and the endings (a–g) to summarise the dream story.

1 One hot, sunny day, the writer and her sister Halima

2 Suddenly, a big dark shadow appeared,

3 Just after that, Dido, the writer's dog, also appeared;

4 The girls jumped on Dido's back and he flew away,

5 Halima took a whistle out of her pocket

6 Then she blew the whistle

7 The cloud they were on disappeared;

a and the writer was frightened.

b were lying on the grass.

c and told Dido to sit on a cloud.

d and the shadow turned into lots of flowers.

e they fell down into the flowers and were not hurt.

f he had grown very big and had silver wings.

g but the shadow chased them.

Use of English: extreme adjectives

SB p.137

1 Match the extreme adjectives in the box with the adjectives (a–j) which have a similar meaning. Use a dictionary, if necessary.

amazed	boiling	enormous	exhausted	fantastic
filthy	freezing	furious	terrified	tiny

a surprised   b angry   c frightened

d big   e small   f tired

g great   h dirty   i cold

j hot

2 Read the Language tip. Then complete the sentences with absolutely or really and extreme adjectives from Activity 1 above.

> **Language tip**
>
> **Making extreme adjectives stronger**
>
> Extreme adjectives contain the idea of 'very' in their meaning, for example, *fantastic* means 'very good', so we have to use the adverbs *really* or *absolutely* to make them stronger, for example, *absolutely fantastic*, *really filthy*.

1 It was the most frightening experience I have ever had; I was *absolutely terrified*.

2 I couldn't believe how hot it was in there; it was _____.

3 It was dirty work and very tiring too, by the end of the day we were _____ and _____.

4 We all thought he would be big but he wasn't. He was a _____ man!

5 Everybody was _____ when we finished first because nobody had thought we could win, and the other team was not pleased at all; in fact they were _____!

Use of English: similes

1 Complete these well-known English similes with the words from the box.

> a picture   a cucumber   a bus   a bird   the hills   a baby

1 I ate too much. Now I feel as big as _a bus_ .

2 My brother can't do anything on his own – he's as helpless as _____ .

3 When I left that place I felt as free as _____ .

4 Throw that hat away – it's as old as _____ !

5 She wasn't worried. She stayed as cool as _____ .

6 They have a lovely little daughter who is as pretty as _____ .

2 Rewrite the sentences in Activity 1 above. Make up your own similes.

1 _I ate too much. Now I feel as big an elephant._ _____

2 _____

3 _____

4 _____

5 _____

6 _____

Check your progress

1 What can you do now?

I can ...

talk about sleep habits and dreams ☐

use different types of adverbs and prepositions ☐

use extreme adjectives ☐

plan and write a story using interesting language ☐

work in a team to design a poster ☐

2 Answer the questions about this unit.

1 What have you enjoyed most?

_____

2 Is there anything you have found difficult?

_____

3 What would you like to learn more about?

_____

💡 My learning

What did you learn in this unit?

3 Soap operas

Reading: comprehension

Read the text about soap operas again and answer the questions.

1 How did soap operas get their name?

_____

2 Which country did the first soap operas come from?

_____

3 Which two radio soap operas does the text mention?

_____

4 What is the world's longest-lasting soap opera called and where is it set?

_____

5 What is *E20* and where can you watch it?

_____

Reading: thinking about the text

Read the text again and answer the questions.

1 Why do you think so many people all over the world like soap operas?

_____

_____

2 The first soap operas were on the radio during the day. Why do you think that there were adverts for soap during the breaks?

_____

_____

Vocabulary: words in context

Complete the sentences with the words in the box. You may have to change the form of some words.

| community | dull | episode |
| forever | set | version |

1 Personally, I find soap operas _____; they are about people's ordinary lives and nothing exciting ever happens in them.

2 *The Archers* has been on the radio in the UK since 1951 and, so far, there have been more than 18 000 _____.

3 The new internet soap opera is _____ in a fashion company in New York.

4 She doesn't want to be a soap star _____; she hopes to act in the theatre in the future.

5 The latest _____ of the programme will only be shown on the internet.

6 People in big cities often come from all over the world: they are international _____.

Use of English: pronouns

SB p.145

Choose the best pronoun to complete the sentences.

1 His shoes are too small. He needs some new [those / of them / ones].

2 The only two people here are you and [me / I / us].

3 Don't forget his suitcases! They're the big black [ones / them / those] over there.

4 I need some new trousers because [these / this / the ones] are too small.

5 Can you see those two boys? My brother is [he / the one / him] on the right.

6 That's not my daughter's coat. [This / Hers / She] is the grey [one / that / it] is on the chair.

Use of English: sentence adverbs

SB p.145

1 Decide if A or B is the correct place to put the sentence adverb in brackets.

1 That actress is a bad choice to play the hero's mother,
   A_____ because she is a lot younger than him
   B_____! (particularly)

2 A_____, although it's about a successful Chinese family in New York, this soap opera is not popular in China B_____.
   (interestingly)

3 A_____, this series, first shown in 1952, B_____ is still popular today and has 10 million viewers. (amazingly)

4 Nobody expected the film to be a success, A_____ because it was made with so little money B_____.
   (especially)

5 Everybody loves Brad because he's tall and A_____ good-looking but,
   B_____, Judd has a much nicer personality. (actually)

6 A_____, he said he never felt comfortable playing Dr Stevens, although it was the role B_____ he was most famous for. (curiously)

2 Look at the sentence adverbs in each sentence in Activity 1 above and answer the questions.

1 In which two sentences does the writer use a sentence adverb to show that what he/she is talking about is not just interesting but surprising?

_____

_____

2 What facts does the writer especially want to make clear in sentence 1 and sentence 4?

_____

_____

Vocabulary: describing soap operas

SB p.146

Complete the text with the words from the box.

> dramatic   dreadful   episode   realistic   relate to   silly   unbelievable

Although lots of people love it and can't bear to miss an [1]_____, personally I dislike the soap opera *California Girls*. To start with, I find it difficult to [2]_____ the characters: they are too beautiful and well-dressed, and also too [3]_____. They have really stupid conversations and spend all their time shopping even though they are supposed to be top high-school students. It just isn't [4]_____. The acting is [5]_____, too, particularly the actress who plays Jessica, the main character. Even when she's playing a really [6]_____ scene – like when she finally meets her father – she always looks and sounds the same! It's also [7]_____ that she's acting the part of a 16-year-old high-school student, when she looks at least 25.

Use of English: question tags

SB p.147

1 Complete the sentences with the question tags from the box. There are two that you do not need.

> are you   aren't you   have you   haven't you   will you
> won't you   would you   wouldn't you

1 You will text me about next weekend, _____?

2 You aren't going to stay inside watching TV all day, _____? Come on, let's go to the park instead!

3 I didn't expect you to finish everything today. You have been working hard, _____? Well done!

4 I know you really want that game, but surely you wouldn't pay that much for it, _____?

5 I don't think you've met my parents yet, _____? Mum and Dad, this is Liz.

6 You must be there to meet him as soon as he comes out of school. You won't be late, _____?

2 Which two question tags from the box in Activity 1 above were not used? Use them to write two sentences of your own.

_____

_____

3 Complete the dialogues with the correct question tags.

1

A: That was a terrible episode, ¹_____? I found the whole thing completely unbelievable. Why did Jessica run away from home for no good reason?

B: You don't think that in soap operas things have to happen for a good reason, ²_____? What is important is a good, dramatic story! That's what keeps people interested.

A: But a story can't be dramatic if it's just silly, ³_____? Personally, I just get bored.

2

A: Ooh, it says here that Tyler Moore, the actress who plays Jessica, is going to leave the show. If she does, the show will lose a lot of viewers, ⁴_____? A lot of people only watch it because of her.

B: Do you think so? Why would she leave? She would never get another role as popular as Jessica in any other show, ⁵_____?

A: Of course she would. She's terribly talented, ⁶_____? People like her get offered roles in films and series all the time.

B: Actually, she's very pretty, but I think she's a terrible actress. And she has never acted in anything else, ⁷_____? I think she's only saying she wants to leave so that the producers of the show will give her more money.

Use of English: conjunctions

SB p.149

Choose the best conjunction to complete the sentences.

1 He became very lazy and kept arriving late to work; [consequently / furthermore] he lost his job.

2 He doesn't look right for the part. [Besides, / However,] he is too young for such an important role.

3 I'm afraid we can't offer you a part in this series. [However, / Therefore] we will consider you for other roles in the future.

4 Although Meg's young, she's one of the best actresses we've had on the show [while / furthermore] Hal is only popular because he's so good-looking.

5 We have already spent all the money we had to make these episodes; [therefore / however,] we will have to stop filming earlier than we planned.

6 We don't have the money to pay Ed a big salary. [Furthermore / While] he's not even a very good actor.

Vocabulary: drama

SB p.150

Complete the review with the words in the box.

> director   dialogue   character   setting   script
> dramatic   dynamic   episode   props

When I was a drama student, I had the opportunity to act in an [1]_____ of
a popular soap opera. I played an unimportant [2]_____ – I was someone's
girlfriend – but I was in some very [3]_____ scenes where lots of exciting things
happened. I only received my [4]_____ a day before the filming so I was worried
that I wouldn't remember my words. The [5]_____ for the scene was outside
a church and I had one short [6]_____ with the actor who was about to get
married. The series had a new [7]_____ and he had not told the actors what to
do. He wanted us to move about naturally but that made me so nervous that I forgot my
[8]_____! I was supposed to give a bunch of flowers to the bride, which was
important because the [9]_____ of this scene was the bride's husband finding a
message hidden in these flowers that he isn't meant to see. Unfortunately, I left the flowers in
the dressing room!

Check your progress

1 What can you do now?

I can …

talk and write about soap operas ☐

use sentence adverbs and question tags ☐

understand people talking about soap operas and TV programmes ☐

use conjunctions to compare and add information ☐

write about my opinions ☐

My learning

What did you learn in this unit?

2 Answer the questions about this unit.

1 What have you enjoyed most?

_____

2 Is there anything you have found difficult?

_____

3 What would you like to learn more about?

_____

Reading: comprehension

SB p.157

Read the text again and choose the correct answer (a or b).

1 What does the limbic system make the body do?
   a react to emotions
   b feel pleasure

2 How does the brain get information from our senses, for example, from our eyes?
   a It receives electronic signals.
   b Our heart beats faster.

3 How does our body sometimes react to danger?
   a Our heart beats more slowly.
   b The hairs on our body stand up.

4 What did the part of the brain called the hypothalamus help prehistoric man to do?
   a become more intelligent
   b react quickly to danger

5 According to Dr Dan, how do our emotions help us to survive today?
   a They help us to choose positive things that make us happy and are good for us.
   b They help us to stay fit and healthy.

6 Emotions can be bad for us …
   a only when they are negative.
   b if they are extreme.

Reading: thinking about the text

SB p.157

Answer the questions with your own ideas.

1 Can you think of a time when you reacted quickly? Describe what happened. What was your reaction?

_____

_____

2 What negative emotions do you think teenagers are affected by most? Why?

_____

_____

Vocabulary: words in context

1 Complete the sentences with the words from the box. You may have to change the form of some words.

> aggression   anxiety   choice   danger   depression
> habit   pleasure   survival

1 She has a _____ of eating chocolate every night before she goes to bed, which isn't good for her.

2 If we know we are in _____, our body will react, for example, our heart will beat faster.

3 You have a _____: either you can stay and fight or you can run away.

4 My sister worries about everything a lot. She needs to control her _____.

5 I love it when people laugh at my jokes – it gives me a lot of _____.

6 Prehistoric man depended on his emotions for his _____.

7 He said he feels sad all the time; I think he is suffering from _____.

8 If you often get angry and want to fight with people, you have a problem with _____.

2 Match the words in the box from Activity 1 above with these verbs and adjectives (a–g).

a choose	*choice*	**b** pleased	_____
c anxious	_____	**d** dangerous	_____
e aggressive	_____	**f** survive	_____
g depressed	_____		

3 Choose the best word to complete the sentences.

1 My parents gave my brother the [choose / choice] between coming on holiday with the family or staying at home alone.

2 You shouldn't show so much [aggressive / aggression] towards the other team when you are playing football. It's only a game!

3 This part of the town can be [danger / dangerous] at night.

4 It's not possible to [survive / survival] more than a few hours in the desert if you don't have enough water.

5 It is always a great [pleasure / pleased] for my grandparents to see their grandchildren.

6 My mother feels [very anxiety / anxious] if my father is home late. She thinks he might have had an accident.

Use of English: impossible conditionals

SB p.159

1 Match the beginnings (1–6) and the endings (a–f) to make sentences.

1 If you had got up a bit earlier,

2 I would have given you a present

3 If only I had worked harder,

4 I think most people would have reacted the same way as you did

5 If she had said sorry,

6 If only you had asked for directions,

a I would have passed the exam.

b I would have forgiven her.

c if the same thing had happened to them.

d you wouldn't have missed the bus.

e if I had known it was your birthday.

f we wouldn't have got lost.

2 Complete the dialogue with the correct form of the verb in brackets.

Sonja: I've just had an argument with Maria. I wish I ¹_____ (not got) so angry with her. I said some terrible things. If only I ²_____ (not lose) my temper!

Alison: What did Maria do?

Sonja: She borrowed my laptop without asking. If she ³_____ (ask) me, of course I ⁴_____ (lend) it to her, but she just took it from my room. There was some work on it that I hadn't saved and now it's lost.

Alison: Oh dear. Was it a lot of work?

Sonja: It was my geography homework. It wasn't very much and I ⁵_____ (not get) so angry if she ⁶_____ (say) sorry straight away, but she didn't. She said that it wasn't her fault. She said that if she ⁷_____ (know) that there was a document open, she ⁸_____ (save) it.

Reading: short texts

SB p.159

Read the email and the handwritten note. Then answer the questions, choosing a, b or c.

1 What is the purpose of Alison's email?
a to tell Maria that she feels sorry for her
b to explain that Sonja can be aggressive so Maria shouldn't feel bad
c to advise Maria to say sorry to Sonja

To:	Maria
From:	Alison

Hi!

I'm sorry to hear that Sonja's so angry with you. She can be a bit aggressive but I think she could have a reason to be cross. You should have told her before you used her computer and you did lose her geography homework. If I were you, I'd apologise and then wait for her to calm down.

2 Why has Chris written the note?

> Andy - thanks for lending me your laptop. I'm sorry I didn't return it sooner but I was having such fun playing games on it - it's so much faster and better than my old one.
>
> Chris

a. because he wants to borrow Andy's laptop

b. because he wants to apologise to Andy for not returning his laptop sooner

c. because he wants to thank Andy for playing games with him

Vocabulary: emotions and feelings

SB p.160

Read the clues and complete the crossword.

Across

1 Will you please stop shouting and c_____ down.

4 Be careful of the dog, it's very a_____ and it might attack you or bite you.

7 I sometimes get terrible feelings of a_____ – if I see someone being unkind to a child it makes me furious!

8 He had an expression of s_____ on his face, as if the whole world amazed him.

Down

2 Most people agree that l_____ for and from other people is what makes us happy.

3 We spend our lives searching for h_____ – nobody wants to be sad.

5 If you often have feelings of s_____ for no reason, which won't go away, you might be suffering from depression.

6 When I saw what he'd done, I really lost my t_____ and shouted at him.

Vocabulary: poetry

SB p.161

Complete the text about poetry with the words from the box.

rhyme	rhythm	pictures	metaphor	verses	poets	literature	similes

Do you like poetry? Some people think that it is difficult and boring, but it's one of my favourite types of [1]_____. I don't think that there are as many [2]_____ as there are other types of writer. There are probably also more people who enjoy writing – and reading – stories, but poems can be fun, too. What I love about poetry is that the sound is so important. A poem can have a [3]_____, just like a piece of music has. This can help you remember it: the beat of the word is like the beat of a drum inside your head. And [4]_____ – using words that have a similar sound, especially at their end – is another thing that makes poems beautiful.

Poems are like paintings as well as like music. They create word [5]_____. When the writer uses a [6]_____ (for example, he or she talks about a 'pale ship in the sky' instead of the moon or 'a broken heart' to talk about extreme sadness) it helps you to see these things in a new way. [7]_____ – when the writer compares something to something else (for example, 'my love is like a red, red rose') – can also surprise you and make you see something differently. I love learning long poems with lots of [8]_____. Whenever I'm bored or waiting for something, I say them in my head.

Check your progress

1 What can you do now?

I can …

understand a text about how the brain works ☐

talk and write about emotions ☐

use a range of abstract nouns ☐

use *if / if only* in impossible conditional sentences ☐

write about regrets and wishes ☐

understand and write about a poem ☐

💡 My learning

What did you learn in this unit?

2 Answer the questions about this unit.

1 What have you enjoyed most?

_____

2 Is there anything you have found difficult?

_____

3 What would you like to learn more about?

_____

5 A healthy future

Use of English: talking about the future

SB p.166

1 Read the statements (1–5) and match them with the definitions (a–e).

1
> I think I'll tidy my room tomorrow.

2
> The lesson finishes at half past ten.

3
> We're meeting outside the hospital after school.

4
> Maybe I'm going to study medicine at university.

5
> Everyone will use chatbots in the future.

Definitions

a a fixed arrangement according to a timetable

b a general intention – something a person wants to do but perhaps he or she hasn't worked out the details yet

c a sudden decision about what to do in the future

d a prediction – what someone thinks will happen in the future

e a definite plan made in advance, often with a specific date or time

2 Read the statements (1–5) in Activity 1 above again. Then match each statement with the correct verb form (a–d).

a present simple tense

b *going to* + verb

c *will* + verb

d present continuous tense

3 Write sentences about:

a A definite plan you have for next week or soon in the future. Give the time and date.

_____

b An idea you have about what you are probably going to do when you are older and finish school.

_____

c A prediction about something you think will happen in the future.

_____

Reading: comprehension

SB p.168

1 Read the text again and decide if the sentences are true or false.

1 Chatbots are designed to help people. True / False

2 Doctors spend a lot of time with people who are not seriously ill. True / False

3 If you are ill, you can go to see a chatbot instead of a doctor to get advice. True / False

4 We will have to give our chatbots lots of personal information. True / False

5 Chatbots will be even better and more useful in the future. True / False

6 In the future, personal chatbots will completely replace doctors. True / False

2 Two of the sentences in Activity 1 above are false. Write out correct versions.

_____

_____

Reading: thinking about the text

SB p.168

Read the text again and answer the questions.

1 How will chatbots continue to develop and get better in the future?

_____

_____

2 What might personal chatbots be able to do for us?

_____

_____

Vocabulary: words in context

SB p.169

Complete the dialogue with the words from the box. You may have to change the form of some words.

| communicate | continually | medical | support | symptoms | treat |

Alice: So, in the future, when we're ill we'll talk to special ¹_____ robots. Is that right?

Caz: Yes, you'll tell the robot your ²_____ in as much detail as you can, explaining exactly what hurts and where. The robot will then decide how to ³_____ you.

Alice: I don't like that! I'd much prefer to ⁴_____ with a human being.

Caz: I think the idea is that robots won't replace doctors but they will ⁵_____ and help them. For example, if a patient is very ill, doctors will be able to use robots to check how they are ⁶_____, 24 hours a day. That's something that machines can do and humans can't.

Vocabulary: multiword verbs with *take*

SB p.169

1 Match the verbs (1–6) with the meanings (a–f).

1 take up (*The new sofa takes up too much space in the living room.*)

2 take care of (*I'm helping my mum to take care of the baby, who is sick.*)

3 take over (*My father hopes my brother will take over the family business.*)

4 take off (*What time does our flight take off?*)

5 take out (*My dad took the whole family out to a restaurant.*)

6 take after (*I take after my dad: we've got the same blue eyes and dark hair.*)

a be like someone else, usually a family member

b fill time or space

c leave the ground and go up in the air

d look after

e take control of something

f take somebody somewhere and pay for him or her

2 Complete the sentences with a verb from Activity 1 above in the correct form.

1 We _____ nearly half an hour late, but landed on time.

2 She has a great sense of humour. She _____ her dad, who loves making people laugh.

3 The farmer is ill in hospital, so who is going to _____ his cattle?

4 After _____ us _____ to the theatre, my grandfather drove us to his house for dinner.

5 On long journeys, when my dad gets tired of driving the car, my mum _____.

6 Thank for all your help and advice, and I'm sorry I've _____ so much of your time.

Use of English: future passive

SB p.169

Complete the texts with future predictions. Use the future passive form of the verbs in the box.

discover	~~drive~~	kill	grow	cover	use

Transport

In the future, you won't need to learn to drive. Cars [1]*will be driven* by robots. All we will need to do is tell them the address of the place where we want to go! New sources of energy

[2] _____ so we won't need petrol any more. Natural energy from the wind and

the sun [3] _____ for power instead.

Food

There will be more people and less available land in the countryside so food [4] _____

in cities. The roofs and even the walls of buildings [5] _____ with plants, fruit

and vegetables. Animals [6] _____ and eaten as they are now because we will have better sources of protein.

Use of English: –ing forms and to + verb

Complete the second sentence so that it means the same as the first. Use no more than *three* words. Use the words given and the *–ing* form or to + verb.

1 I think it's a good idea to take responsibility for your own health.

I believe _in taking_ responsibility for your own health.

2 It doesn't seem possible that we could talk to a robot instead of a doctor

I can't imagine _____ to a robot instead of a doctor.

3 I asked my father if he would try this new treatment and he said yes.

I asked my father and he is willing _____ this new treatment.

4 I don't want to hear any more about how great technology is.

I'm tired _____ how great technology is.

5 My parents won't buy me a more expensive computer

My parents are not prepared _____ me a more expensive computer.

6 Getting up is less difficult when I've had eight hours' sleep

It's easier _____ when I've had eight hours' sleep.

Vocabulary: words in context

SB p.170

Complete the text about voxpops with the words from the box. You may have to change the form of some words.

effect	find out	insist	public	trust	valuable

Voxpops are a way of [1]_____ how the [2]_____ feels about something. A reporter goes out into the street and interviews anyone who agrees to talk to him or her. We are not quite sure why, but people often seem to [3]_____ a voxpop reporter and be willing to talk to him or her. Being asked for their opinion can have an extraordinary [4]_____ on some people: once they start talking, they don't want to stop! They will [5]_____ on talking to the reporter even when he or she thanks them and tries to end the conversation! One thing is certain, voxpops are a [6]_____ way to discover what people think.

A healthy future

Vocabulary: biology

Read the clues and complete the crossword.

Across

3 To take air in and out of the body (in order to stay alive) is to **b**_____.

6 Our **b**_____ is the organ in our body that controls everything and we use it to think.

8 The smallest units or parts of a living thing are **c**_____.

10 **D**_____ is when your body turns the food in your stomach into things your body can use.

11 The organs in your body that take in air and let out air are your **l**_____.

12 **B**_____ is a red liquid that flows round your body.

Down

1 **O**_____ is a gas in the air which all humans need to stay alive.

2 The gas that humans breathe out of their bodies is **c**_____ **d**_____.

4 The organ in your chest that sends blood round the body is your **h**_____.

7 **N**_____ feed your body and help it to do its job and grow.

9 The **l**_____ is a large organ in the body which helps to clean the blood.

Check your progress

1 What can you do now?

I can …

talk and write about healthcare in the future ☐

use different future forms ☐

understand voxpop interviews ☐

My learning

What did you learn in this unit?

use the –ing form and to + verb correctly ☐

understand a text about body organs ☐

2 Answer the questions about this unit.

1 What have you enjoyed most?

_____

2 Is there anything you have found difficult?

_____

3 What would you like to learn more about?

_____

Vocabulary: music

SB p.176

Find the words in the wordsearch to complete the sentences.

m	u	s	i	c	i	a	n	d	g
u	e	t	h	i	n	q	p	o	n
s	v	c	k	r	s	u	p	w	o
i	i	s	f	u	t	e	i	y	r
c	o	n	c	e	r	t	a	b	c
a	l	v	x	a	u	c	n	o	h
l	i	s	r	g	m	k	o	q	e
v	n	n	j	l	e	c	s	t	s
x	y	b	d	e	n	a	l	r	t
z	o	p	o	l	t	l	m	i	r
c	o	n	d	u	c	t	o	r	a

1 People make music by playing an **i**_nstrument_.

2 A person who plays an instrument is a **m**_____.

3 You need to have some **m**_____ talent to be able to play and sing.

4 A **v**_____ is an instrument with strings that you put against your neck and play by moving a bow across the strings.

5 A **p**_____ is a large instrument with black and white keys.

6 People go to a **c**_____ to hear music being played or sung.

7 An **o**_____ is a big group of people who play different instruments and make music together.

8 A **c**_____ is a person who stands in front of a group of musicians or singers and directs them, using his or her hands.

Use of English: prepositions

SB p.177

1 Match the beginnings (1–8) and the endings (a–h) to make sentences.

1 He's always been very keen	**a** *of their project.*
2 How did they react	**b** *of dogs?*
3 Is she good	**c** *with me?*
4 A good teacher really cares	**d** *to each other.*
5 Is he really afraid	**e** *on joining an orchestra.*
6 My friends made a big success	**f** *at sport?*
7 Why do you always disagree	**g** *about her students' success.*
8 They look very similar	**h** *to the news?*

2 Complete the second sentence so that it means the same as the first sentence. Use the words in brackets with a preposition and a verb in the –*ing* form where necessary. Use no more than *three* words.

1 He's liked playing music all his life. (keen)

He's always been *keen on playing* music.

2 It doesn't matter what I say, he never agrees. (disagree)

He always _____ what I say.

3 Your voice doesn't sound very different from mine. (similar)

My voice sounds _____ yours.

4 Singing in front of an audience makes me feel scared. (afraid)

I am _____ in front of an audience.

5 My younger brother plays the piano well. (good)

My younger brother is _____ the piano.

6 For some musicians, the only important thing is to make money. (care)

Some musicians only _____ money.

7 You are going on tour for the first time: does that worry you? (anxious)

Are you _____ on tour for the first time?

8 I won the school music prize and this makes me feel proud. (proud)

I am _____ the school music prize.

Vocabulary: word building

SB p.177

1 Complete this list.

a fear   adjective: *afraid*

b reaction   verb: _____

c anxiety   adjective: _____

d similarity   adjective: _____

e disagreement verb: _____

f fame   adjective: _____

2 Complete the sentences with a word from Activity 1 above and the correct preposition.

1 She has a terrible _____ _____ flying and won't go anywhere by plane.

2 My friend is _____ _____ being the best footballer player in the school. Everybody knows who he is and wants him in their team!

3 My new phone is very _____ _____ yours – but mine is pink!

4 I had a _____ _____ my best friend and now we aren't speaking to each other.

5 The exam was very difficult and I feel _____ _____ my results – I don't know if I have passed or not.

6 I am going to tell her my ideas, but I don't know what her _____ _____ them will be.

Vocabulary: words in context
SB p.178

Complete the sentences with the words from the box. You may have to change the form of some words.

| background   impact   lead to   understanding   unique |

1 I've never heard anything like this in my life. It is absolutely _____!

2 Hearing the world-famous orchestra play has had a big _____ on me: I have decided to become a musician.

3 If you want to increase your _____ of music and how it works, then join this course.

4 Playing in the orchestra often _____ the chance to travel and meet musicians from other countries.

5 It is not easy to do well in life if you come from a poor _____ but it is possible.

Reading: comprehension
SB p.179

Read the text about El Sistema again and complete the sentences with *one* word.

1 *El Sistema* is a music _____.

2 It was started in _____ in 1975 by a man called Jose Antonio Abreu.

3 He wanted to give children from _____ families the chance to learn music.

4 He believed that learning music could help these children to change their lives and give them a better _____.

5 Any child can go to *El Sistema* because the classes are _____.

6 The children enjoy themselves learning music and they also feel _____ while they are there.

7 The older children in *El Sistema* often become the _____ of the younger children.

8 *El Sistema* has its own _____ which has become famous all over the world.

Reading: thinking about the text

SB p.179

Read the text again and answer the questions.

1 How does *El Sistema* help children from poor families to have better lives?

_____

_____

2 How does studying at *El Sistema* help young people to become more understanding of each other?

_____

_____

Use of English: reflexive pronouns

SB p.180

1 **Choose the best word to complete the sentences.**

1 It was a great concert last night. Your mother and I really enjoyed [myself / ourselves].

2 You are very wet, children! Please use those towels over there to dry [yourself / yourselves].

3 A snake will only bite you in order to defend [itself / themself].

4 Can you help me? I have cut [myself / yourself] badly with a knife.

5 The children taught [themselves / itself] to play the musical instruments.

6 She had just told him he hadn't passed the exam and he was feeling very sorry for [himself / herself].

2 **Complete the sentences with a reflexive pronoun.**

1 Nobody helped him; he did it by _____.

2 There are drinks and biscuits on the table over there. Tell the students to help _____.

3 The cat jumped out of a high window and hurt _____.

4 Our parents couldn't pay for singing lessons so we had to teach _____.

5 May I introduce _____? My name is Jose.

6 My sister often talks to _____.

1 Match a word from box A with a word from box B to complete the sentences.

A | double-bass   ~~percussion~~   lead   ticket   world |

B | tour   singer   ~~section~~   player   price |

1 The _percussion section_ was led by the famous Yoruba drummer, Oga Alayande.

2 We all admired the _____ _____'s deep, rich voice.

3 During the final song, the _____ _____ played with such energy that he broke one of his strings.

4 Considering the high _____ _____, we had expected a better performance.

5 This was the band's first concert on their _____ _____.

2 Put the words in order to make sentences.

1 definitely recommend / new band. / this exciting / I would

_____

2 some / there were / Unfortunately, / technical problems.

_____

3 the old songs. / we enjoyed / Unsurprisingly, what / most were

_____

Check your progress

1 What can you do now?

I can …

use prepositions with adjectives, verbs and nouns ☐

use different reflexive pronouns ☐

understand an article about a music school ☐

talk about my experience of music and music I like ☐

write a review of a concert ☐

My learning

What did you learn in this unit?

2 Answer the questions about this unit.

1 What have you enjoyed most?

_____

2 Is there anything you have found difficult?

_____

3 What would you like to learn more about?

_____

End-of-year review

Vocabulary: word hunt

Can you remember four words or phrases you have learned that are:

1 Unit 9: nouns connected with survival camp

2 Unit 10: nouns connected with treasure hunting

3 Unit 11: words connected with business

4 Unit 12: extreme adjectives

5 Unit 13: adjectives for describing TV programmes / films

6 Unit 14: abstract nouns for emotions

7 Unit 15: nouns for organs and body parts

8 Unit 16: musical instruments or jobs related to music

Vocabulary: a crossword puzzle

Read the clues and complete the crossword.

Across

1 An **e**_____ is a person who starts a business.

5 S_____ are feelings or problems in our body that show a certain illness.

7 When something is **v**_____, it is worth a lot of money.

8 A **n**_____ is a very bad dream.

9 R_____ is a feeling of happiness and comfort because nothing is worrying you.

Down

2 An **e**_____ is one programme of a series shown on television.

3 S_____ is when someone or something continues to exist after a difficult or dangerous time.

4 The talking in a book, play or film is the **d**_____.

5 A **s**_____ is a phrase that compares one thing to something else, using the words 'like' or 'as'.

Use of English: passive tense review

Change these sentences to the passive form. You may sometimes need to add the word by.

1 Where do people speak Spanish?

Where is _____ ?

2 I don't know where they are going to hold the next Olympic Games.

I don't know where the next _____.

3 Tourists were ruining the peaceful countryside.

The peaceful countryside _____.

4 I don't know if anyone will meet you at the airport.

I don't know if you _____.

5 Nobody has told him what he needs to do next. He _____.

6 Her relatives were lying to her. She _____.

7 They had given him a prize but they took it away again. He _____.

8 The teachers are not giving her enough help. She is not _____.

Quiz: *Focus on ...*

Can you remember these facts from the Focus on ... sections in the Student's Book?

1 Five abilities sportsmen and women are always trying to improve: **a**_____,

   sp_____, **ba**_____, **sta**_____ and **str**_____.

2 The name of the pirate in *Treasure Island* is _____.

3 The Silk Roads were a network of _____ _____ which linked the _____

   and the _____.

4 The longest line of latitude around the middle of the Earth is called the _____.

5 A person who writes for TV is called a _____. The text they write is called a _____.

6 Poems often _____ – they have words with a similar sound. They also have

   a _____; the words follow a beat like a piece of music does.

7 The gas humans need to stay alive is called _____; the gas our lungs breathe out

   is _____.

8 Musical instruments that you blow into in order to play them are
   called _____ _____.

Writing: my year

Think about what you have learned this year in English and complete the sentences.

1 My favourite topic in the book was _____ because

   _____.

2 I think that I am good at _____.

3 I think that I need more practice in _____.

4 This year in English, I am proud of myself because I have made progress with

   _____.

5 Next year in English, I would like to learn how to _____.

Focus on grammar

1 Present tenses [9Uf3, 9Uf4, 9Uf6, 9Uf8]

a. The present simple tense
- is made with the simple form of the verb, or verb + –s for 3rd person singular (*he, she, it*)
- is used to talk about general facts, habits and timetabled events in the future

b. The present continuous tense
- is made with *am / is / are* + *–ing* form of the verb
- is used to talk about actions that are continuing in the present, happening around now and for future plans

c. The present perfect tense
- is made with *have / has* (*not*) + past participle of the verb
- links the past and the present. The action takes place in the past but there is always a connection with *now*.

  The present perfect tense has three uses:
  - for something that *has happened recently* (often with *just*)
    The players have just arrived.
  - for something that started in the past and is still not finished (often with *for* and *since*)
    Scientists have known about Komodo dragons since 1916.
    They have studied these strange creatures for over 100 years.
  - for an experience (often with *ever* in questions and *never* in answers)
    Have you ever seen a Komodo dragon?
    No, I've never seen one in real life but I've seen them on television.

  We often use time adverbs with the present perfect.
  - yet / so far = at any time up to now   *I haven't seen the new film **yet**.*
  - lately / recently = a short time ago   *Have you seen any new films **lately**?*
  - ever / in all my life = at any time up to now   *I've **never** seen a better film **in all my life**.*

d. The present perfect continuous tense
- is made with *have / has* (*not*) *been* + *–ing* form of the verb
- links the past and the present but shows that the action is continuing or has just finished
  He is tired now because he has been working all day.

See Section 4 for the passive form of these verb tenses.

2 Past tenses [9Uf3, 9Uf6, 9Uf7, 9Uf8]

a. The past simple tense
- regular verbs are made with the verb + *–ed* but many common verbs have irregular past forms
- is used to talk about finished events in the past

b. The past continuous tense
- is made with *was / were* + *–ing* form of the verb
- is used to talk about actions that were continuing in the past

c. The past perfect tense
- is made with *had* (*not*) + past participle

- is used to talk about an earlier past (that is, two steps into the past)

    She went to live with her parents after her husband had died.
  d. The past perfect continuous tense
    - is made with *had* (*not*) *been* + *–ing* form of the verb
    - is used to talk about an earlier past but also shows that the action was continuing

      It had been raining all day so everything in the garden was wet.

See Section 4 for the passive form of these verb tenses.

3 Future forms [9Uf5]

There are a number of ways to talk about the future in English:

	will arrive	
	will be arriving	
She	is going to arrive	tomorrow evening at 19:00.
	is arriving	
	arrives	

All of the sentences are correct. However, there are some differences in the use of each.
  a. **will** + verb is used for
    - sudden decisions (often with *I think*)

      I think I'll talk to my teacher tomorrow.   *I'm tired. I think I'll go to bed.*
    - predicting or guessing

      In the future we will all go to university.   *I think it will rain tomorrow.*
    - future events you are certain about

      It will be my birthday next week.   *The teacher will be here in a minute.*
  b. **will be** + *–ing* form of the verb
    - actions or events which will be continuing at or around a time in the future

      At lunchtime today, she'll be jogging in the park.
  c. **be going to** + verb is used for
    - something we have decided to do, or plans

      I'm going to fly to London tomorrow.   *He's going to visit us on Friday.*
    - future events we have evidence for

      Look at the sky! It's going to rain.   *Look at the time! We're going to be late.*
  d. The **present continuous tense** is used for
    - fixed or firm plans – often with a time, date or place

      I'm meeting him at six o'clock at the airport.   *They're arriving on Monday.*
  e. The **present simple tense** is used for
    - things which are timetabled to happen in the future

      His plane arrives at 08:30.   *What time does the exam begin tomorrow?*

4 Passive forms [9Uf3, 9Uf5, 9Uf6, 9Uf8]

- A passive can be used with any of the verb tenses: we use the verb *be* in the appropriate tense + the past participle. Some examples:

PRESENT SIMPLE PASSIVE:	The film	is	chosen	by the manager.
PRESENT CONTINUOUS PASSIVE:	The book	is being	written.	
PAST SIMPLE PASSIVE:	The car	was	washed	by my sister.
PAST CONTINUOUS PASSIVE:	We	were being	followed.	
PRESENT PERFECT PASSIVE:	A dog	has been	found.	
PAST PERFECT PASSIVE:	The rubbish	had been left	on the pavement.	
FUTURE PASSIVE:	Cars	will be	driven	by robots.

- We use passives when we don't know, we don't want to say or it is not important who did something. Passives are often used in reports.

  My money was stolen. (I don't know who took it.)

  A window has been broken. (I don't want to say that I broke it.)

  A lot of rice is eaten in Asia. (It is not important who eats it.)

- We use a passive to continue talking about a topic that has been introduced

  English is a useful language. It is used all over the world.

- When we use a passive and want to say who did something, we use *by …*

  A telephone call was made by my mother.

5 Modal verbs [9Uf9]

- Modal verbs add meaning to main verbs. They are not used about facts. They are used to express ability, possibility, certainty, requests, suggestions, necessity, and so on.

- The modal verbs are: *can, could, may, might, must, shall, should, will, would, ought to*. We also use *have to* and *need to* for the same purpose.

- Modal verbs only have one form. They do not add *–s, –ing* or *–ed* (or *do / does / did* for questions).

- Past modal verbs use modal + *have* + past participle of the verb.

- To express certainty and uncertainty about the past, use *must / mustn't have, can / can't have, could / could have* and *might / mightn't have*.

  "He might have left already." "No, he can't have left: his car is here. He must have gone upstairs."

- To express regret and criticism, use *should / shouldn't have*.

  He shouldn't have taken her computer. I should have asked her first.

6 Conditionals [9Uf10]

Conditionals are sentences with two clauses: an *If* clause and a main clause. They are used to talk about the results of something happening which hasn't happened.

a. **The likely conditional**

- *If* + verb in simple present tense: *will / won't* + verb
- is used to talk about real and possible situations which are likely to happen.

  If it's sunny tomorrow, we'll go for a picnic.   *If I have time, I'll call him this afternoon.*

b. **The unlikely conditional**

- *If* + verb in simple past tense: *would / wouldn't* + verb
- is used to talk about the result of things which are not likely to happen

  If it snowed, I would be surprised.   *I'd be very happy if I had my own plane.*

- also used to express a wish and to give advice

  If I had lots of money, I would buy my mother a car.   *If I were you, I would see a doctor.*

c. **The impossible conditional**
- *If* + verb in past perfect tense: *would / wouldn't have* + past participle of verb
- is used to talk about things that happened in the past and are impossible to change
  If you had arrived earlier, I would have taken you to out to lunch.
- is used with *I wish* and *if only* to express regrets and wishes about the past.
  If only I had arrived on time, the teacher wouldn't have been so angry.
  I wish I had arrived on time.   *I wish I hadn't made her angry.*

d. *Unless* (meaning *if not*) can replace *if* in all three conditional structures.
  Unless he is very ill, he will be at school tomorrow.
  I wouldn't have phoned him unless you had suggested it.

7 Reported speech   [9Uf11]

- When we use reported speech, the place, time and speaker have usually changed from the time and place the words were spoken. For this reason we often have to change the verb tenses, pronouns and "time and place" words.
- The tenses change like this:

tense change	speaking	reported speech
present simple ➔ past simple	"I **walk** to school."	He said he **walked** to school.
present continuous ➔ past continuous	"He **is working**."	She said he **was working**.
past simple ➔ past perfect	"I **played** football."	He said he **had played** football.
present perfect ➔ past perfect	"We **have missed** school every day."	I said we **had missed** school every day.

- Examples of how time and place words change:

now	➔	then
today	➔	that day
yesterday	➔	the day before
tomorrow	➔	the next day
next week / month / year	➔	the following week / month / year
last week / month / year	➔	the week / month / year before
here	➔	there

- When we report on a situation that has not changed (the time and place are still the same) then we do not have to change the verb tense. This happens when
  - we repeat something immediately after it is said
    "He is arriving soon."   *"What did you say?"*   *"I said he is arriving soon."*
  - we are talking about something which is still true or always true:
    "My name is William."   He said his name is William.
    "Water boils at 100°C."   The teacher told us that water boils at 100°C.
- The most common verbs for reporting are *said* and *told*. There is an important difference in the way they are used.
  - We use *told* when we say **who** somebody is talking to.
    *Adu **told his wife** that there was a problem*   *I **told you** that I would help.*

○ We use *said* in other cases.

    *Adu **said** that there was a problem.*   *I **said** that we would meet later.*

● To report a command, use *told* + noun / pronoun + *to* + verb.

    The teacher said, "Cal, sit down."   *The teacher told Cal to sit down.*

● To report a request, use *asked* + noun / pronoun + *to* + verb.

    Jan said, "Help me carry this box, please."   *Jan asked me to help him carry a box.*

● To report a *Wh-question*, use *asked* and the word order of a statement (not a question).
Do not use a question mark.

    He said, "Where are you going?"   *The man asked where I was going.*

● To report a *yes / no* question, use *asked* + *if*.

    My mother said, "Are you feeling well?"   *My mother asked if I was feeling well.*

8 Question forms [9Uf3]

a. **Yes / no questions** do not include a question word and can be answered with *yes* or *no*.

● We make *yes / no* questions by putting the auxiliary or modal verb before the subject.

    Do you leave home before 8 o'clock?   *Can he play the piano?*

● For *yes / no* questions with the verb *be*, we put the verb before the subject.

    He's French.   ***Is he** French?*

    They weren't there last night   ***Were they** there last night?*

b. **Question-word questions** start with a question word: *why, what, which, when, where* or *how*.

● The word order after the question word is usually the same as for yes / no questions.

QUESTION WORD	AUXILIARY / MODAL	SUBJECT	VERB
Where	**have**	*you*	**been**?
What	**had**	*they*	**been eating**?

● The question words *who, what, which* and *how much / many* can be used to make
questions about a subject or an object. When the question is asked about the object, we
use an auxiliary or modal verb before the subject as usual. However, when the question is
asked about the subject, we do not use an auxiliary or modal verb and the word order is
the same as for a statement.

SUBJECT	VERB	OBJECT	
Kalu	*told*	*Sani.*	*Who did Kalu tell?* (answer = Sani, OBJECT)
			Who told Sani? (answer = Kalu, SUBJECT)
The dog	*is chasing*	*the cat.*	*What is the dog chasing?* (answer = the cat, OBJECT)
			What is chasing the cat? (answer = the dog, SUBJECT)

c. **Indirect questions** are used when we want to be very polite.

● We make an indirect question by putting it inside another question or statement.

    Direct question: *What time did he arrive?*

    Indirect questions: ***Could you tell me** what time he arrived?*

    ***I wonder** if you could tell me what time he arrived.*   ***Do you know** what time he arrived?*

d. **Question-tag questions**

● Question tags are short questions that we put on the end of sentences, especially in
spoken English. They are not usually real questions. The speaker usually knows the
answer and is asking the listener to agree.

● We use the same tense in the main sentence and the tag.

- If the main part of the sentence is positive, the question tag is negative.

  *She's a teacher, **isn't she**?*   *You live in London, **don't you**?*

- If the main part of the sentence is negative, the question tag is positive.

  *You don't know him, **do you**?*   *They aren't playing, **are they**?*

- When the main sentence has any part of the verb *be*, then we use it in the tag.

  *He **is** late again, **isn't** he?*   *They **weren't** here, **were** they?*

- When the main sentence has an auxiliary or modal verb (*have, do, can, must*, and so on), then we use it in the tag.

  *He **has** arrived, **hasn't** he?*   *They **shouldn't** see us, **should** they?*

- When the main sentence is in the present simple or past simple tense and does not have *be*, an auxiliary or a modal, we use *don't/doesn't/didn't* in the tag.

  *He plays football, **doesn't** he?*   *They went home, **didn't** they?*

9 –ing form and to + infinitive   [9Ut6, 9Ut7]

a. We use the *–ing* form of the verb

- after prepositions   *I dream about becoming a vet.*   *We left after saying goodbye.*
- after some verbs   *He suggested talking to you.*   *He avoided sitting in the sun.*
- We can also use the *–ing* form of the verb:
  - as the subject or object of a sentence

    Cooking is my hobby   *He loves swimming.*
  - as an adjective

    This is an amusing book   *It was a frightening experience.*

                                                                    [9Ut6]

b. We use *to* + infinitive

- after adjectives   *I'm sad to hear the news.*   *We're happy to stay for dinner.*
- after some verbs   *I promise to help you.*   *He appears to be happy.*

10 Quantifiers and modifiers   [9Uf1]

- Quantifiers are small words that tell us about quantity, for example: *some, many, a few*.
- Some quantifiers can be used only with countable nouns and some only with uncountable nouns. Others can be used with both.

Quantifiers used for both countable and uncountable nouns	Quantifiers used for countable nouns only	Quantifiers used for uncountable nouns only
some	many	much
any	a large / great number of	a great deal of
a lot	few / a few	a large amount of
lots of	both	little / a little
all of	each	
none of	either	
more	neither	
enough	several	
plenty of		

- We can add the words *very*, *so* and *too* in front of both countable and uncountable quantifiers to give more information.

  There's too much rubbish in the streets.   *Very few people have jobs.*

- We can use *all of*, *half of*, *twice*, and so on to tell us more about the amount of something.

  We have been waiting all this time.   *Half of my money was stolen*

11 Adverbs

[Ug3], *[Ug4]*

- Adverbs give information about *how*, *where*, *when* or *how often* an action happens, or *how certain* we are that it will happen.

- Adverbs that tell us *how often* or *how certain* go before a main verb and after a modal, or auxiliary verb or the verb *be*.

  I sometimes read in bed.   *He probably lived in town.*

  He doesn't often go.   *She is clearly late.*

- Adverbs that tell us *how*, *where* and *when* usually go at the end of a sentence. There can be more than one adverb in a sentence. The order for these adverbs is *how – where – when*.

  *They played **well in the match yesterday**.*

- Sentence adverbs describe a whole sentence or clause.

  ***Unfortunately**, our train was late.*

  *Nobody expected the film to be a success, **particularly** as it was made with so little money.*

12 Comparing

[9Uf2]

- Comparisons with adjectives can be made stronger or weaker using these structures:

  (not) *as / as*   *just as / as*   *much* + comparative adj + *than*   *slightly* + comparative adj + *than*

  I'm not as tall as you. *He's much stronger than he was.* *He's slightly stronger than he was.*

- Comparisons with adverbs can be made stronger or weaker using these structures:

  (not) *as / as* *just as / as*   *far less / more* + comparative adv   *much* + comparative adv + *than*   *slightly* + comparative adv + *than*

  This computer doesn't work as quickly as it used to.

  It rained much more heavily than before.

  Jan drives far more carefully than her dad.

- We use *like* or *as* to say one thing is the same as another. These structures are called similes.
  - verb + *like* + noun phrase: *She's like a mother to me.*   *It disappeared like ice in the sun.*
  - *as* + adjective / adverb + *as*:   *It was as cold as ice.*   *He ran as fast as a cheetah.*

13 Relative clauses

[Ut9]

- A **defining relative clause** tells us about the noun. It is an important part of a sentence. If we take it out, the sentence may not make much sense.

  *The doctor **who you saw yesterday** is away today.*

- A **non-defining relative clause** gives us extra information about the noun. We can take it out of the sentence and still understand it. We use commas to separate it from the rest of the sentence.

  *The doctor, **who is now over 70**, is resting.*

- **Relative pronouns**
  - We use *who* to refer to a person: *I saw a man **who** has a wooden leg.*
  - We use *which* to refer to an animal or a thing: *There is the monkey **which** bit me.*

- We can use *that* to replace *who* and *which*:

  I saw a man **that** *has a wooden leg.* *There is the dog* **that** *bit me.*

- We use *why* to give reasons. *The reason* **why** *I like her is that she always has time to help.*

- We use *where* to talk about a place. *This is the place* **where** *I live.*
- We use *when* to talk about a time. *2015 was the year* **when** *my brother was born.*

- We use *whose* to talk about possession. *This is the boy* **whose** *coat I borrowed.*
- We can also use *which* to talk about the whole of the previous sentence.

  My uncle gave me some money, **which** *was kind of him.*

  We missed our train and had to come home by taxi instead, **which** *was annoying.*

14 Pronouns   [9Ut4, 9Ut5]

- Pronouns take the place of nouns, for example: *she, them, ours.*
- **Demonstrative pronouns** are used
  - to show what we're talking about by pointing at something

    That *is my son.*   **Those** *are my shoes.*
  - to refer back or forwards to something in a text

    The film stopped and **this** *is what made everyone angry.*

    If **that** *is what you want for your birthday, I can take you to the game.*
- **Reflexive** pronouns are used when we want to refer back to the subject of the sentence.

  I gave **myself** *time to relax.*   *Did you teach* **yourself** *English?*

  He cut **himself** *with the knife.*   *She helped* **herself** *to some cake.*

See Section 13 for relative pronouns.

15 Conjunctions   [9Uf8]

- Conjunctions connect two ideas in a sentence. Some always go between the two ideas but others can also go at the beginning of the sentence. If the conjunction is at the beginning, use a comma between the two parts.

  Although *I like flying, I didn't enjoy that flight.*
- We use *furthermore* to add information.

  He is intelligent; **furthermore** *he is honest.*
- We use *so that* and *(in order) to* to explain a purpose.

  I studied hard **so that** *I would do well in my exam.*

  We opened the window **(in order) to** *let some air in.*
- We use *consequently* and *as a result* to talk about results.

  His parents worked all over the world; **consequently** *he grew up speaking several languages.*
- We use *although* and *however* to contrast two ideas:

  Although *I don't have a lot of free time, I always make time to read in the evenings.*

  The book was interesting; **however**, *parts of it were difficult to understand.*
- We use *while* and *whereas* to balance two contrasting ideas.

  While *I don't enjoy comedy, my sister loves it.*

  I always read quickly, **whereas** *my friend reads slowly.*